IF YOU CAN'T FAIL,
It Doesn't Count

To my dad, who wanted to write his own book but ran out of time.

Thank you for helping me write mine.

Introduction

This book is remarkable.

I really do mean that. It is remarkable because, in writing it, I did not settle for *good enough*. If I had settled for that, it would just be another book. But this one isn't just another book.

It is my book.

It is me.

This book is about me being vulnerable and putting my ideas out there for you to read and possibly connect with. The reality is that you might do neither. Honestly, this book isn't for everyone. If it was, there would be nothing remarkable about it.

That's why I wrote it for you.

Knowing that you have picked up this book and are spending the time to see what it is all about tells me that you are most likely the type of person who is remarkable too. You being remarkable has nothing to do with reading my book. Not one bit. I say that you are

4

remarkable because you are curious enough to peek at a title like this one, *If You Can't Fail, It Doesn't Count.*

Just think about that.

Why do anything if it doesn't count? Why do anything if you don't run the risk of failing?

If you come up with a good answer for either of these questions, put my book down and read something else. But until you do, keep reading. There's more to failing than you might think.

Failure is a scary thing. That's why we make it out to be the bad guy. Really though, it isn't.

In fact, we need to fail more often. We need to fail . . . hard.

If we never fail, it means that what we are doing has already been done or isn't worth doing in the first place. If we never fail it is because we are comfortable where we are, not moving. If we never fail, it means that we don't truly want to succeed. That might be fine for you if you are simply here to exist.

But if you are here to live with a fury, you need to fail.

This book might fail. You might not read it. If you do, it might not connect with you. I could pay over $500 to get a *Kirkus Indie* Review, and have them tell me it's rubbish. Customers of Amazon.com could write cynical things about me or my work for all to read on this title's purchasing page. You could even find errors of one kind or another and generalize it as a lack of my literary skill.

Truthfully, there is nothing that I can do to stop any of that. And really, I'm okay with it.

I wrote this book with passion and gusto. I read it and read it and read it, grooming through every single word and punctuation mark to make sure that it tells the story that I want to tell in the precise way that I want to tell it to you.

Nevertheless, that is not the most remarkable part of this book. This book is remarkable because I launched it. You are reading this right now and conjuring up your own thoughts and ideas because I was willing enough to write, to publish, to sell, and to let go of the outcome.

Yes, I wrote this book. But it is not mine anymore. It is yours. Before that, it was someone else's.

I imagine that you came across my book by word of mouth. If so, it is because someone else has connected with the ideas that I share here. That alone makes this all worth it. That alone makes this count.

If you are curious enough to see if this will connect with you, then read on. I thank you for your courage. If you like what you read, if something about it moves you, please share this with a friend.

We are all on the verge of something big. And something big is very high up. If you are here with me, I have a few words of encouragement for you . . .

Whatever You Do, Look Down

Ideas are dangerous. That's quite possibly why so many of us keep them to ourselves. If we let them out, bad things might happen. Occasionally, when we can muster up the chutzpah to put our ideas on display, we do it with a safety net . . . just in case we fail.

The best ideas don't need a safety net. They risk failing. Most ideas fail. Some ideas, the remarkable ones, risk failing from a quarter of a mile up in the air.

Take one of Philippe Petit's ideas.

He's a tightrope walker. However, the New York City Port Authority would call him a tightrope dancer. That's because Petit didn't just walk across tightropes. He danced across them.

Perhaps Petit's most famous performance was back in 1974 across the most iconic buildings in our collective American mind. New York City's Twin Towers, then part of the recently built World Trade Center.

Philippe Petit, in his mid-twenties at the time, took a team of co-conspirators and sneaked to the top of the Towers with their equipment in tow. They had Philippe's 26-foot long balancing pole, a 450 pound steel cable, a large rope, fishing lines, and a bow and arrow that they would use to get the rope and fishing line from one building to the other. It was across these supports that Petit would shimmy the 450 pound three-quarters inch thick steel cable to the opposite anchor point.

Until the time was right for Petit and his crew to do that, they stashed their supplies a few steps away from where Philippe would step off the skyscraper and over the chasm.

Laughably, nobody noticed. That was the plan until their return and performance the next day.

August 7, 1974, was *the* next day. It was the day that Philippe's idea was going to get noticed. Atop one of the two tallest buildings in the entire city, Philippe Petit stepped off the edge. He stepped off of the building, 1,368 feet above New York City, and onto a steel cable less than an inch thick.

In front of his ambitious friends and the unsuspecting world, Philippe walked along the cable the 200 feet between both Towers without a safety net or harness. When he finally made it across the void, he turned around and did it again.

Phillippe walked across his Twin Tower tightrope a total of eight times. For 45 minutes, this man on a wire put on an aerial show that captivated onlookers below. He didn't just walk on the cable. He *jumped* on the cable. He *danced* on the cable. And at one point, he lay on his back, looking at the clouds, and had a conversation with a nearby bird all while on less than an inch of cable.

Phillippe Petit did not fall.

He certainly could have though. He walked from tower to tower without a safety net to catch him. What if something went wrong? He was willing to risk that.

That's why Philippe Petit is still talked about over 30 years after his audacious stunt. He was ultimately vulnerable. He believed in his ability to walk out on a limb (or a cable), and he was willing to show the world that he was not concerned with what might happen if things didn't work. All he cared about was focusing on things working.

This is a short book about what happens when things don't work and why we should start welcoming that more often. We've been taught to be winners. We've been told that winners never fail. And it's great to think that . . . if you're a loser.

Winners fail all the time. If they didn't, they wouldn't keep trying to win. That's where the title for this book comes from. It's not my opinion. It's a universal principle; it's a law. The verbiage is credited to Seth Godin. But the application of this concept is yours and mine. If you can't fail, it doesn't count.

The problem is that we often fail to fail. That's a lot of wasted time and energy. Why do we do that to ourselves?

It's all because of a lizard.

Godzilla, or is it?

Godzilla terrorized Japan in 1954 while the memory of
the bombing of Hiroshima was still in the country's
consciousness. Directed by Ishiro Honda and produced
by Toho, the original *Godzilla* depicted a giant monster
which had been mutated by nuclear radiation ravaging
the Land of the Rising Sun.

Honda's idea was to play to Japanese filmgoers'
emotions by creating a culture of fear that hit close to
home. *Godzilla* most certainly did just that.

Some critics were very upset at the insensitive timing of
the movie's release. Apparently, their animosity wasn't
enough to stifle 27 sequels. It would have had to have
been greater than our natural inclination toward being
scared. To be realistic, that is a lot.

We are programmed to be afraid. Since birth, we cry. That's our way of saying that something is not right. It's a natural response to things not being the way that we expect them to be. To be controlled by this type of fear, however, is not natural. In fact, it's often the result of Hollywood-like exaggerations playing out on the set that is our brains.

Labeled the "lizard brain" by psychologists, this tendency to succumb to fear and avoid danger is hardwired into our grey matter. This fear-control center in humans is very similar to the brains of Godzilla and other lizards. You can find it atop the brainstem in the back of your head. Brain scientists call it the amygdala. And they've discovered that the amygdala serves two main purposes: survival and sex.

The amygdala, or lizard brain served us well when we were hiding from prides of lions on the Serengeti. Update: We're not on the Serengeti anymore. We live in houses in suburbs and metropolitan areas with grocery stores and fast food restaurants on the corner. Our survival is safer than it used to be.

As for sex, we still have that. We just have it in more comfortable quarters now.

Yet, we still let fear consume us. That hasn't changed. What has changed about our fear is what we are now actually afraid of.

Are we afraid of a real-life Godzilla, or something else?

Anonymous

When I married my wife, she mounted a decorative plaque on our kitchen wall that reads, "What would you attempt to do if you knew you could not fail?" It is credited to no one. Perhaps the author was not brave enough to step forward for fear of shame and criticism. It is quite a ridiculous query.

I've seen this quote marketed on magnets, t-shirts, vanity license plate covers, mouse pads, mugs, and more. Interestingly, it's just a question. It's a question, though, that engages people emotionally because we think that the answer is beyond our control.

Wouldn't that be nice to really be able to succeed without failing? I wish that could happen to me.

It can't, and it won't. This book is about why you should be glad about that. As hard as it is to swallow, we need to fail and fail more often. We just need to figure out how to do it the right way.

If we fail and then hang our heads in shame, we are failing horribly, horribly wrong. That way of responding to failure is what pressures us to stop what we are doing and promise to never try something like that again. How silly.

If you get nothing else out of this book besides what I'm about to say, get this. Failure is not the termination of

15

possibility. It is permission to continue pursuing a worthy cause.

Things worth achieving without the adversity of failure are of low importance and even lower value to our lives. Our lizard brains do not realize this. They are too concerned with our safety and preservation. That explains why, when facing risk, we start stirring up the worst possible outcomes. Often, if not always, when we think about worst case scenarios, we are wrong.

Dead wrong.

If we knew we could not fail, we would never attempt anything worth achieving. Nothing would have the same value. That is why the question should change. Instead of "What would you do if you knew you could not fail?" We should start asking "What *are* you going to do?"

And do it.

Imagination and Stomach Electrodes

It got us to where we are today, and our lizard brains won't back down without a fight. We are failure averse creatures. If it served us well once, it will serve us well again. There's only one problem.

We don't do the same things today that we did thousands of years ago. Where our day-to-day objective then was to acquire food and secure shelter, today, our main objective is freedom. It's not the freedom to do whatever we want. That is not actually freedom. It is the freedom that comes with being in control of ourselves, the freedom to select what we do and how we do it.

Ironically, our early brains sought security so that we could be more free. Now we are free. We just can't seem to give up our earlier tendencies.

Fortunately, we have more to our cerebral selves than our bitter amygdala. Unlike lizards, both mutant and real, we have a brain system that works in concert to enable us to dream, imagine, and create. Our brains are the only ones that can do this. That's how we have stirred up ideas for our amygdala to be afraid of.

Explaining our ability to imagine could fill an entire book by itself. This book is not going to do that. So, simply know this. Fear comes from one part of the brain. One part.

It requires much more to imagine than to shirk in fear. Perhaps that is why so few of us let ourselves imagine. It requires more work and more energy. It's more of a risk of being wrong. If we imagine and fail, it reflects back on us. If we play it safe and do nothing, there's no harm done.

At least, that's what we think.

It's like exercise sold on TV. Instead of buying a membership to a local gym, doing the research needed to develop a fitness plan, and then hitting the weights, we are lured into the products on TV that offer the best results with the least amount of effort. That's easier. If we go to the gym, we might give up. Actually, most of us will. That's embarrassing. But if this abdominal electrode doesn't work, it's the product's fault, not mine.

When we can limit the work we do, there is nothing to be afraid of, except the reality that we're not doing anything at all.

Let's Redefine Fear

It is the anxiety about something not turning out the way you expect it to be. Anxiety is the experience of failure before it ever happens. Now, doesn't that sound counterproductive?

Can you imagine how boring life would be if everything turned out to be exactly how we anticipated it in our minds? There would be no surprises. No excitement. No innovation or change. There would be nothing to drive us to keep going, no reason for us to move.

Yes, some things will get in our way. But that is half of the fun with moving.

One Of the Best Moments of My Life

I was riding in a U-Haul moving truck while my mom drove to the end of the parking lot in our apartment complex. She was going to turn the vehicle around. And as she did, my mother turned it very smoothly. She had to. There were fences, a dumpster, and a fire hydrant that she understandably did not want to run over or through. I remember seeing her so aware of the headlights, the tires, and the rear of the truck.

But she forgot about the overhead carriage on top. That is until it clipped the corner of an aluminum carport.

The entire structure snapped like a twig and fell to the ground like a broken down cardboard box, smashing the cars that were parked directly beneath it.

That was certainly not what I had expected to happen that day. Judging by the sailor's language coming from my sweet mom, she didn't expect that to happen either. But I'll never forget the experience. You can't buy something like that.

Things turning out differently from what we expected isn't always a bad result. Naturally, that would mean that failing isn't always bad either. So, why are we so afraid of failing then?

We are afraid because failure surprises us with new challenges. We are afraid of projects or risks that force us out of our comfort zones by presenting new paths for us to decide between. Part of the adventure of life, though, is deciding which path to travel down. Things will get in our way. That is inevitable. So should we go down the well-trodden path, or try our luck where no one has travelled before?

Follow the *Red* Brick Road

When Dorothy wakes up in *The Wizard of Oz* and finds herself in Munchkinland she is immediately told what to do. Follow the yellow brick road. That's an imperative with no choices to make. Once she got to the end, she was able to meet with the cacophonic wizard just in time to come to her senses from her unconscious dream state.

The Wizard makes for a good metaphor for our fears, being smaller than Dorothy was led to believe.

This is one of my favorite movies. But I've always wanted a screenwriter to create an alternative storyline to *The Wizard of Oz*.

 If you've ever seen the movie, you might have noticed that as the Yellow Brick Road eddies out of Munchkinland on its way to Oz, there is a second road, a red road, that nobody in the Lollypop Guild mentions. How would the story be different if Dorothy had chosen which path to take for herself?

22

It certainly wouldn't have fit in the song, but I imagine it would have made for an incredibly interesting story.

Two Questions

We need to start asking ourselves two questions every single day. *What am I afraid of not working?* and *What am I afraid will actually work?*

You're already having a difficult time answering the second one.

It's the first of these two questions that we dwell on though. It drives us to stay where we are and keep on doing what has proven to be safe. When we focus on this question, we color in the lines. Paradoxically, the second question can be just as debilitating. *What am I afraid will actually work?*

If our big ideas take flight and connect with real people, we're going to have to admit that we were wrong about our self-doubts and capabilities. If they soar, we can no longer be martyrs. Can you handle accepting that you created something like this? It's time to stop being humble, at least with yourself.

You're going to respond differently depending on which of these two questions you are asking yourself. The answer to one will irritate you, while the answer to the other will agitate you. Both will make you move. If you're irritated, you'll move away. If you're agitated, you'll move forward.

Think just about today. Think about how you would prefer to be spending your time. I'm not asking you what you would attempt to do if you knew you could not fail. That is not a realistic question. I'm asking you to consider this . . . are you afraid of failure actually *failing*?

A Stubborn Hymnal

Steven Silver was a scientist working for 3M labs when he made one of the biggest mistakes of the company's life. Silver had been given the task of creating a new, stronger adhesive that could be used as an alternative to what 3M already had on the market. He set to work in his laboratory creating a concoction that he supposed would do the trick. Surprisingly, what Silver had brewed up did the exact opposite. It barely stuck to anything at all. His newly created adhesive held things together, but it could be easily removed.

He didn't throw it away though. In fact, the idea stuck around (pun intended) for at least ten more years until a member of a church choir got tired of his hymnal markers falling off of the pages.

Arthur Fry was also a scientist at 3M. He had been placing paper markers on the pages of his hymnal to make sense out of what he was singing, but they always seemed to slip off of the pages, and Arthur Fry would lose his place. That's when he remembered the failed adhesive that his colleague, Steven Silver had stumbled upon a decade earlier.

He used that adhesive to lacquer the edges of his paper markers and stuck them to the pages in his hymn book.

Finally, the book markers stayed in place. They could also be easily removed and reapplied elsewhere without damaging the thin paper pages. How convenient? How unexpected?

What Steven Silver had created and Arthur Fry had found a purpose for has now become one of the most popular business supply items in the world. The Post-It Note is used by everyone in every industry and has been digitized for computer use as well.

What was once a failure soon failed at failing, eventually revolutionizing the way people remember things.

There are a few lessons to be learned here, two of which I will share with you. First, you don't actually know what failure looks like. You might think you do, but you don't. You are simply afraid of things not matching the picture that you have painted in your mind.

Second, don't give up on mistakes. Pursue them long enough to determine whether they are dead ends or Red Brick Roads leading to somewhere or something you never knew about.

People pay good money to learn the lessons that others have discovered by pursuing mistakes. They pursue gurus and know-it-alls to impart their secret wisdom. Think about any successful businessperson, innovator, author, or artist and you will find someone with a long history of pursuing mistakes. Think of anyone with a long history of pursuing know-it-alls, and you'll find them still sitting in the bookstore.

The secret to success isn't going to be found from a guru; it's going to be found from a lifetime of experience and a lifetime of failure. Stop wasting that.

Head West!

This reminds me of a man who was forced to file for bankruptcy after a failed cartoon series he produced in Kansas City, where he lived. At 22-years old, this man chocked it up to a loss and packed up his things to move to California with a *go-west* mentality. In search of his own gold rush, he left Kansas City for Los Angeles with a cheap suitcase that he packed with a shirt, underwear, socks, and a few drawing materials. Just enough to keep him busy.

Once there, he realized that California was filled with animators who were much more skilled than he was, so this man decided to turn his attention to acting. While pursuing gigs in Hollywood, this ambitious young man realized that while there were a lot of animators in the Golden State, there were no animation business headquarters in California. So he decided to start his own with the help of his brother.

With nothing else going for them, what could they possibly lose?

28

The man that I'm talking about was named Walt. The animation studio that he and his brother built was named The Walt Disney Company.

I'm sure you can fill in the rest.

Just don't forget the lifetime of mistakes that one of the world's greatest innovators continued making and the failures that he continued experiencing. Also, don't forget that he let none of them stop him from achieving his dream.

Disney is credited with saying, "I think it is important to have a good hard failure when you're young. I learned a lot out of that. . .Because of that, I've never had any fear in my whole life when we've been near collapse and all of that."
For Walt, there's been a lot of "all of that."

But not enough to stop him.

We Don't Have It In Our Budgets to Do Nothing

Both Steven Silver and Walt Disney saw failure for what it really is, an opportunity. They were not born with this lens in place, which means that we can view failure through it too. How? Well, here's the first step.

Make mistakes daily and own them.

What's the worst that could happen?

I'm not talking about fatal mistakes like speeding through a red light or throwing water on a grease fire. I'm referring to mistakes where the cost of failure is less than the cost of doing nothing. You don't need to understand advanced economics to comprehend this. The fine print here is that the cost of doing nothing is usually quite high. It's most likely too high for you to be able to afford doing nothing at all.

So let's start doing something. You've got nothing to lose. It's already being lost.

Molehills

I hate to admit it, but oftentimes we refuse to act on our ideas because of molehills. Real molehills are mounds of loose soil that appear on top of our beautiful grass when a mole is repairing its burrow. The mound that is raised by the mole is waste material from its burrow underground.

Most of us treat it as such, and we spend an entire Saturday trying to get rid of the mole so that we can have our beautiful yards back.

This reminds me of Bill Murray's relentless pursuit of a similar pest in the 1980 movie *Caddyshack* which ends with him detonating dynamite and blowing up a golf course green to once and for all get the gopher. If you've seen the movie, you know that the critter gets away, making all of Bill Murray's character's work for naught.

The escapade is funny because we do it too. We might not work on golf courses, but we certainly spend our time and energy (two of our most valuable resources) chasing after what seems to be tantalizing problems.

As the idiom goes, we make mountains out of molehills. And we let them get in our way. The interesting thing about real molehills is that they can actually be quite valuable if you only look at them in a different light.

I'm not a gardener, but I know people who are. They've taught me about a branch of ecological design called permaculture. Permaculture is a synergistic approach to gardening which asks, "Where does this element go?" The answer helps develop sustainable architecture from natural ecosystems.

To those who practice permaculture gardening, a molehill is a welcome sight. The process that a mole goes through to remove the dirt that has infringed on its burrow creates a fine potting soil for humans to use. It's the mole's claws that do this to the dirt. Molehills also aerate and till the soil in your yard, adding to your lawn's fertility.

An astute gardener recognizes the benefits of molehills for what they truly offer; resources to help our gardens grow.

In the pursuit of our goals, we will come across molehills. At least now, we can choose how to view them. Either make them into impassable mountains, or scoop them up to make our gardens grow.

Stripping Away the Inessential

Jo was an imaginative little girl who absolutely loved stories. Her creative mind was an obvious character trait of hers as a young lady. Jo's parents embraced it for a while, but knew that she would one day have to grow up and start living in the real world that they lived in.

Jo's parents were incredibly poor, and they certainly didn't want their daughter to end up in the same place that they found themselves. They wanted Jo to eventually grow up and enter the work force with the skills that she would need to make her money. Imagination wasn't one of these skills and would soon need to be left to child's play.

As she grew up and continued to let her imagination roam freely, Jo's parents continually pressured her to take life a bit more seriously and prepare for a trade job after graduating from college. College was an education that neither of Jo's parents had ever received.

Like you and me, Jo did grow up. And she did in fact graduate from college. Just not in the field that her parents had hoped for her. Jo had kept her study of classic literature a complete secret from her mom and dad. She knew they wouldn't approve of her chosen field of study.

For the record, Jo's parents did have good intentions. They wanted everything that they didn't have for their spry daughter. They had an idea of life as they had both wanted to live it, and they wanted that life for Jo.

Jo had other ideas for herself, however. She wanted something different. It would take her a while to find it. She would have to endure heartbreak, loss, and some serious setbacks. But Jo would eventually find something different.

Seven years after graduating college, now 28 years old, Jo found herself as a single mother, the result of a very short-lived marriage. She also found herself living poor, incredibly poor. Her parents' worst nightmares had come true.

Scared, defeated, and dejected, Jo was as poor as you could possibly be without quite being homeless. She was poor like her parents were poor, but Jo was not poor of imagination and heart.

In the evenings, she took her daughter for walks to help her fall asleep. It allowed Jo to let her mind wander. A distressed mind has a lot of places to go. Often, the two of them would end up in a cafe as part of their nightly strolls where Jo's daughter would sleep and Jo would do what she had always done best, imagine.

I would guess that she imagined a better life for herself and her daughter. She most likely resented past decisions and suffered feelings of guilt. We all do that. Quite possibly, Jo also became depressed. Something that a lot of us do as well.

Still, she imagined. That didn't depress her. The imagining she focused most on was the story she was writing. She had come up with the idea for it one day while riding on a passenger train.

Having hit rock bottom, she decided to strip away everything that was inessential and instead focus on finishing the only thing that mattered to her.

Writing her first book.

Once it was finished, Jo sent it off to twelve different publishers. And twelve different publishers rejected Jo's book until the daughter of one company's owner read the manuscript and persuaded her dad to publish it. She had loved the story that it told and thought that other kids her age would enjoy it too.

On June 26, 1997, *Harry Potter and the Philosopher's Stone* (the European title) was published. As of this writing, Jo (known otherwise as J.K. Rowling) is a billionaire. More importantly, her decision to pursue her passion in light of having failed at so many other things in life has inspired children and adults around the world to read books again, and to imagine.

Since the first print run in 1997, the Harry Potter books have sold nearly 500 million copies. That is so many that, as of this writing, it ranks as the bestselling book series of all time. I doubt that even Jo's parents could have dreamt up something like this for their daughter.

It was one of Jo's most iconic characters, Albus Dumbledore, in *Harry Potter and The Prisoner of Azkaban* who said, "Happiness can be found, even in the darkest of times, if one only remembers to turn on the light."

When so many other things were trying to keep hers turned off, Jo turned on her light. Now, it's bright enough for people around the world to see.
To think that it was once only child's play.

What's Your Idea? That's Your Art

Everyone has an idea. Whether old or new, there is something that burns inside you. Perhaps light? I call it art. And I call you an artist.

We are so enamored with innovative thinkers and authors who write about creative revolutions. We seek opportunities to meet leaders in their given field. And we are willing to read biographical tomes of people like Richard Branson because of the successes that we have come to associate with their art.

The only reason they are intriguing to the world is because they actually launched their ideas.

Acting on your passions is a limited commodity because most of us don't think that our ideas are worth the energy we would put into shipping them. That's why the ideas of those who do launch them is so valuable. They spent the time and energy so ship their work. They must have special powers that we don't have. That explains it perfectly.

Who am I? we ask.

The answer should be reason enough to unleash your idea by taking the first steps to create your art. That is the super power that those *other* people have. They start, and they finish. That's it.

So, what are you going to start?

Of Course There is Try

The notion that you either do or you don't is narrow minded. It's also wrong. Stop believing it right now. It assumes that you've mastered everything. You either perform or you don't. We must recognize the real value and meaning of trying something new. It doesn't even need to be something new to the world. Perhaps, it's just something that we haven't been able to do before.

Felix Baumgartner set the altitude record for a manned balloon flight, parachute jump from the highest altitude, and greatest freefall velocity all on the same day after he jumped from a capsule at the edge of the atmosphere, 24 miles above the Earth's surface.

He did this October 14, 2012, as the world watched online. The most vividly breathtaking scene from his Red Bull Stratos jump was the moment, after ascending to the edge of space, that Felix opened the hatch to his one man capsule, stepped out onto a small deck, and looked down over the curvature of the world with nothing but black in the background.

No man or woman had ever skydived from that high. No one had ever tried.

Felix wasn't concerned with just the height of his jump. He was also focused on the speed. He was trying to become the first person to break the sound barrier without a vehicle to help him do it. And he was trying to do that on this jump.

It wasn't a do or don't do scenario. Plenty of variables played into this project, some of which were beyond Felix's control. The Red Bull Stratos jump was an attempt. It required Felix and his entire team to try something that had never been tried before.

As if he were falling into his own bed, Felix Baumgartner belly flopped off of the one man capsule which was tethered to a giant helium balloon on the edge of outer space. Looking like an astronaut who had ejected from his space shuttle, Felix's body began racing toward Earth in a space suit and helmet.

And the world watched, not knowing what on Earth (or above it) would happen.

Free falling for over four minutes, the success of this attempt was as suspended as Baumgartner, himself. Trying something that had never been done before, there were a lot of unknown possibilities.

Things went smoothly until they didn't. At one point, Felix started spinning. The speed and the force of the fall started throwing his body in circles. But having trained for just that, Baumgartner successfully regained control of himself and his jump.

The first success of this jump was exactly that, jumping. Though an extreme athlete by profession, putting yourself in a position where you will be careening toward the hard earthen surface faster than anyone has ever experienced takes some guts. That is putting it mildly.

The second success was careening toward the Earth faster than anyone had ever done before. He fell at a speed of 834 mph.

The third success was something that no one had ever seen happen, a sonic boom caused by a human body. On the Red Bull Stratos jump, Felix Baumgartner conquered a new frontier by breaking the sound barrier without the help of a vehicle. It was just him, gravity, and sound waves that couldn't keep up.

Once his feet safely contacted the New Mexican desert, Felix dropped to his knees and threw his hands up into the air triumphantly, the fourth success.

At the outset, Baumgartner didn't know whether he would do what he had set out to do that day. There was no way of knowing what would happen. Everything could have gone horribly wrong. Preparations were made to study out every single aspect of a jump like this beforehand. Nevertheless, no one had ever done it before.

Still, Felix Baumgartner tried.

I Didn't See that Coming

We need to understand that failure is nothing more than unexpected results. We've painted a picture of the outcome in our minds, and the eventual reality does not look like our initial visions. This creates a feeling of disappointment at first. We have to admit that we were wrong. And wrong is bad.

Or is it?

Nothing new was ever discovered by someone proclaiming, "I knew it!". This reeks of expectation and an absence of mistakes. Without mistakes we would have no art. We would have no light. We would have no cars, or plastic, or books, or flight, or computers, or solar panels, or Facebook.

Science, math, and history are all great tales of people who "didn't see that coming." They are shared experiences of those with the audacity to try something new while being okay with their expectations not being

44

met. Their ideas were ugly ducklings, and history chronicles the people who stuck with them.

Where this might be crippling to those of us not willing to go out on a limb, it is invigorating to those of us who do. We owe our evolution as an intelligent people to chutzpah.

There are endless examples of I didn't see that coming moments throughout history. Each one is unique. Whether they still matter today depends on what happened next. Whether they influenced history is a result of whether the person involved reacted or responded.

Always respond. Always.

The Bank of Experience

"Brace for impact!" were the only words spoken by the airplane's captain. That's never a good sign.

Three minutes after taking off from La Guardia Airport in New York City en route to Charlotte, North Carolina, a flock of Canadian Geese flew directly into both engines of US Airways Flight 1549. Passengers onboard recalled hearing sounds similar to the backfiring of an engine. One passenger toward the back of the cabin even saw fire.

This was certainly an *I didn't see that coming* moment for Chesley Sullenberger, the pilot of the Airbus 320. But Chesley was ready, even if he didn't initially realize how ready he was.

While passengers were hyperventilating, panicking, crying, and praying, Chesley Sullenberger took control of the situation in the cockpit of an airplane with no power. That's a situation where very little is actually still in your control. What you can control is how you respond.

After discussing the possibilities with Air Traffic Control of either returning to La Guardia or landing at a nearby airport in New Jersey, the reality that neither was possible with how quickly his plane was descending sank in. Chesley had to make a decision, and he had no time left to make it.

With nowhere else to go, Sullenberger decided to land his large airplane in the frigid Hudson River right between Manhattan and New Jersey. It wasn't exactly the most remote landing strip, but it was quite possibly the safest one available.

Sullenberger knew there were ports for boats nearby in the Hudson that would be able to respond to the crash and help rescue the surviving passengers.

Flying, or rather *falling*, merely 900 feet over the George Washington Bridge, Chesley later remarked that this moment was, "the worst, sickening, pit-of-your-stomach, falling through the ceiling" feeling that he had ever experienced.

Fortunately for him and his passengers, this wasn't Chesley Sullenberger's first flight. He had amassed more than 40 years and 20,000 hours of flying experience in his career by the day that US Airways Flight 1549 lost power.

That's over 40 years of deposits in the bank account of experience. One by one, each of Sullenberger's deposits accrued until, on January 15, 2007, he had sufficient funds to make an incredibly large withdrawal. He was going to land his plane.

As he continued to fall ever faster toward the Hudson's wakes, Chesley Sullenberger took each necessary step to ditch the plane. He lifted the nose of the airliner right before impact. The rear end of the Airbus hit first, ripping a gaping hole into the cargo hold. Once the rest of the plane had touched down in the freezing water, Sullenberger, who had survived, called one order over the intercom, "Evacuate!"

Flight attendants rushed to help the passengers to exit the plane as the cabin filled with river water. Either onto the wing or the evacuation slide that doubled as a life raft, all of the passengers went.

The last person to exit the aircraft was the captain, Chesley Sullenberger. He was sure to make two trips up and down the aisle of seats to be perfectly positive that all passengers had made it out safe.

All 155 of them did.

In terms of getting his passengers from New York to North Carolina, Chesley Sullenberger failed. The outcome that he had planned on failed to meet his expectations. There is no possible way that he saw an emergency crash landing in the Hudson as his plane took off from the runway that day. But because of his willingness to embrace failure, his crew's ditch landing has come to be considered the most successful ditching in aviation history.

Now, Chesley is retired. He travels around the world to speak on airline safety. And people everywhere refer back to his successful crash landing as *The Miracle on the Hudson*. No one has ever called it *The Failed Flight to North Carolina*.

Why would they?

So What About Me?

You might not be an airline captain. You might not even be responsible for anyone else but yourself. The fact that you are at least in charge of you is reason enough to act.

You are of unquantifiable value. There is no way you can deny that. Keeping your ideas from the world is selfish. Regardless of what it is that you want to create or start, you do not have the right to keep it to yourself. You have been entrusted with empowering the rest of us with whatever it is that you have to offer. And I know that it is great.

Your contribution to our interconnected world can have an impact beyond your scope of realization. If you can launch your art by nothing more than pure will, do that.

What Will Can Really Do

Viktor Emil Frankl was an Austrian psychiatrist. His career did not give his life the meaning that he has become known to embody. It was his time in a Nazi concentration camp that did. Viktor Frankl was a Jew. Like you and me, he was also human. There is no limit to what humans can will themselves to do.

On October 19, 1944, Frankl and his wife were processed as prisoners into Auschwitz concentration camp. Shortly after that, Viktor and his love, Tilley, were separated and sent to slave in different camps. They would never see each other again. Tilley Frankl, Viktor's wife, died alone in Bergen-Belsen.

Frankl didn't just lose his wife to the cruelty of the Nazis. He lost almost his entire family.

Viktor's mother was exterminated in a Nazi gas chamber, the fate of many Jewish prisoners. His brother perished doing slave labor in a Nazi-operated mine.

It would have been easy and understandable for Viktor to give up. Many in his situation did. Viktor, though, didn't. Instead, Viktor Frankl sought out the meaning of life in every moment of the Nazi's Hell on Earth. Talk about optimism! It was through this pursuit that he discovered that life never ceases to have meaning, even in the direst moments and in death.

In his book, *A Man's Search for Meaning*, Frankl tells of a march through the harsh conditions in Auschwitz as Nazi soldiers herded their captives like cattle with thrusts from the butts of their rifles. A fellow prisoner, whom Viktor was leaning on for support as they marched, made a comment about their wives and how he hoped that, wherever they were, they did not have to experience this same sort of hardship.

Frankl's mind immediately turned to thoughts of his beloved Tilley as he continued to trudge through the mud. It was then that an epiphany inspired his resiliency.

The salvation of man is in love and through love. If even caught in the pit of despair where simply living is the greatest success, man can achieve fulfillment in the contemplation of his love.

That's really all that Viktor had, the memories of his love. But it was those memories that would ensure his survival and ability to tell his story upon his reclamation from Auschwitz and the Nazis.

It is chronicled in his transformative book, *A Man's Search for Meaning*, which I highly recommend reading.

Though Viktor Frankl had his home, his possessions, his career, and his family ruthlessly taken away from him. They could never take his will.

Why, then, give up yours?

What If You Do Nothing?

If the greatest attainable success for you right now is simply living, I applaud you for your tenacity and courage. I am humbled and honored that you have chosen to read this book. It might be a risk in itself. The silver lining of your situation is that taking daring risks will be low cost with a great opportunity for success.

If you are not sitting at rock bottom, why waste any more time? Your cost of doing nothing is so much greater than willing yourself to actualize what you love. Your time here is finite, and it's ticking away. Stop rationalizing why you shouldn't be the artist you were

54

created to be. Stop making excuses for why your grand ideas won't work.

You are too blessed to be stressed with the dead end of what-ifs.

It's your lizard brain. And it does a great job answering what-if questions for you. Unfortunately, it rarely gives you the right answer. It makes mountains out of molehills. Your amygdala exaggerates the dangers of failing in order to protect itself. It's very nearsighted. Your potential is a distant blur.

Consider these two questions: *what if you launch your great idea?* List all of the positive things that could possibly happen.

Now, *what if you do nothing?* List all the ways that your life will be better by inactivity.

Which list is more promising to you? Go for that one.

Just Did It

Unless you live in the Lost City of Atlantis, you have seen their slogan. *Just do it*. It's canvassed on every single product and advertisement that Nike has ever produced. The company recruits elite athletes to endorse this simple call to action. And it's worked. In a multi-billion dollar sports industry, *Just do it* and Nike reign supreme.

When Dan Widen penned "Just do it" the year was 1988, and I was one. Every year since, the world has been being told to *Just do it*.

So, why hasn't anyone done it yet?

I've always thought that if Adidas or Reebok wanted to catch up in this one man race, they should market an ad campaign with the slogan *Just did it.* Wouldn't that inspire a much more powerful emotion, one of accomplishment, resilience, and triumph?

We are much the same when it comes to accomplishing things that we create for ourselves. *Just do it* is the attitude that leads to failed New Year's resolutions and regrets. *Just do it* has left more books unpublished than could fill an entire library. It has left that many mountains unclimbed. It has left that many albums unrecorded. And *Just do it* has left that many dreams unlived.

Just did it is the attitude that leads to more possibilities.

I really like *Just did it.*

The Anyone Elses

You might agree with me. You might even think that what you've read up to this point is great or inspiring. You might also be saying *nice, but that wouldn't work for me.*

Why not?

It's worked for others. Some of the most successful people in the world were born outliers, but none of them are mentioned here. They are rare. That's why they are outliers. The others that I am referring to here are like you and me. They're real people. So, why, then, won't it work for *you*?

Perhaps it is because doing away with the inessential and focusing your energy on your art seems like breaking the rules. We've all grown up learning that rules are not meant to be broken and that if they are, we will be punished. In some instances such as theft and murder, punishment is the rule and hopefully always will be.

But rules, my friend, are breakable. When they don't make any sense, break them to pieces.

Being punished for being inspired? Who's going to punish you? If someone does, why waste your time working for or associating with that person in the first place? They are not going to add value to your life.

They're not going to help you get to where you want to be. They are not going to understand or appreciate you or what you have to offer. Instead, they will most likely do the opposite of all of this and drag you back down to self-deprecation and compliance.

Keep moving up, and never stop. Like fog that has darkened a valley, the world above the haze is breathtaking.

The world craves innovators whether we are aware of that fact or not. You were not created any less equal or invaluable than anyone else. The anyone elses who have launched their ideas realize this, and they act on this informational advantage. They refuse to defer to the outliers. More often than not, geniuses are not the ones with the high I.Q.s. They're the ones with information that others don't have.

Having an informational advantage in life is a rather great thing to have.

Playing With the Wrong Ball

There is a video on YouTube of a little league American football team and a play that caught everyone off guard. If you are familiar with the rules of football, this will make complete sense to you. If you aren't, bear with me here.

As both teams met at the line of scrimmage, the pee-wee-sized quarterback approached his offense and got set behind center (the player who snaps, or hands, the ball to the quarterback to begin a play). Anxiously, the opposing defense watched and waited for the snap of the ball. That was their signal to go.

As the quarterback peered left and right, making sure that his teammates were in their correct positions the center casually stood up with the ball in hand and turned toward the quarterback, curiously handing him the ball.

"Coach, we have the wrong ball!" the quarterback hollered over to the sideline.

"What?" the coach called back as if he couldn't clearly hear his captain.

"We have the wrong football!" the quarterback shouted.

"Bring it here!" the coach commanded in a frantic hurry to find the right game ball. How could he have been so stupid as to have sent his team onto the field with the wrong ball?

The quarterback walked toward the sideline as his coach beckoned him to hurry up. All the while the defense stood in place confused, and they watched, waiting for the game to resume.

Two things were made very clear as the quarterback drew closer to the sideline with the football in hand. The first was that the game wasn't going to resume. The clock had been running the whole time. The second was where the real game ball actually was.

It was in the quarterback's hand.

The defense realized this too late as the offensive coach, unveiling his grandest trick play, hastily yelled "GO!". This was the signal to drop the charade. Much to the opposing team's chagrin, the quarterback had tucked the ball in the crook of his arm and sprinted along the sideline, untouched, into the end zone for a very legal score.

Obviously, the scoring team had an informational advantage over their competition. Having read the league rules on game play beforehand, their coach realized that there was no specification for how the center must get the ball to the quarterback to begin a play. Conventionally, the center snaps the ball through his legs and into the quarterback's outstretched hands.

Whether through the center's legs, snapping it farther back to a gunslinger in a shotgun formation, or by standing up, turning around, and casually handing the ball to the quarterback, all were fair. The offense knew this. They were the only team that did. But the defense was made well aware of it too.

No rules were broken by this play. The advantage the offense held was by initiative. While the rest of the league played by what the official rules said to do and to not do, the team mentioned here played by what the rules didn't say. And they won.

We're very busy making sure that we are living by the rules. Whether at school, at work, or in society, we are expected to walk the line, or else. We don't have to break every rule to get what we want.

But often, what's left unsaid is more instructive than what we're told we can and cannot do.

We Just Happen to Sell Shoes

Tony Hsieh doesn't play by his industry's rules. It's made all the difference for him and his company. If you've read any recently published books about organizational management or business leadership, chances are great that you know who Hsieh is. If you've ever ordered shoes online, you probably know of his company as well.

Zappos is the leader in online shoe sales. This is because of their initiative. When Tony Hsieh started Zappos in 1999, he relied on the drop-ship model of doing business. Drop-ship is where customers place orders through Zappos, Zappos sends the orders to the distributors with whom they have contracted, and the distributors ship the orders to the customers. No inventory needed. No mess to clean up. More money for less work. That sounds really nice for an entrepreneur.

Well, not to Hsieh. Perhaps he's just not like other entrepreneurs. Something was missing from how Zappos' CEO wanted to do business. Hsieh and his team were making money, lots of it, but they didn't have a connection with their customers which was worth more to Hsieh than the money ever is.

So Zappos changed, and they risked a lot by doing it. They flipped their drop-ship model and put the customer experience over their bottom line instead of the other way around. They cut out the distributors which accounted for 25% of their total revenue, a huge risk, and supplied their own inventory instead.

What happened? The customer experience improved, and Zappos happened to reach over two billion dollars in gross merchandise sales. Obviously, they would need more room to store inventory.

By general business acumen, this was not a wise move to make. Tony Hsieh just isn't a general businessman. He's a mover. He put people first just like all great movers do. And it paid off. I doubt that he read that advice in a business book, at least not in a general one.

The positive results of launching a new business model weren't simply in terms of revenue and customer experience. The business culture and employee morale at Zappos experienced a significant boost as well.

With one glimpse into Zappos' headquarters it becomes apparent that individuality and initiative are embraced in the workplace. So, it's not *just* about the customer. It's about everyone.

Employees at Zappos are moved by happiness and fun instead of money. Okay, that's not entirely true. If you should be hired by Zappos and decide that it's just not for you while still in your training period, Zappos will let you quit and pay you to do it.

Their feelings are that if you don't enjoy being part of the Zappos family, then that disconnect will negatively affect the customer experience that you provide. It will take away from your ability to move others.

In the long run, it's a lot cheaper to pay for you to find something better to do than to pay you to do what every other shoe company is doing. In the long run, you'll be happier doing something else.

Isn't being happy what the long run is all about?

Something Better to Do

That might just apply to all of us, whatever our situations in life are. It will inevitably end up being a lot cheaper for you to find something better to do than settling with "good enough."

Good enough is safe. Good enough is understandable. Good enough is within our control. Unfortunately, good enough isn't good enough. If it were, we wouldn't need to be motivated to do it. We would act on conviction and passion alone.

There's a shortage of both in the human race, not because we do not have the capability to be driven. We are simply too apprehensive to move. Instead, we are offered rewards to accomplish tasks that serve someone else. Bonuses. Raises. Extended vacation time. Promotions. You name it. All of these are there to fill the void of conviction and passion. They're there to make up for the absence of art.

Tony Hsieh and Zappos understand that. They've created a working culture that taps into passion and fun instead of corporate bank accounts. An employee can be motivated by money in the short term, but eventually she will want more until there is no room for more and the employee goes somewhere else, unhappy to boot.

Happiness is scalable. Money is not. Zappos moves people with happiness. If a shoe sales company can drive itself to the top of its industry by pursuing happiness, can you?

Of course. But it requires some short circuiting.

If You Don't Follow Your Passion, It Will Destroy You

I don't blame you for being driven by money and other temporary, often material, rewards. I am too. There are a lot of things that I can think of doing with a truckload of money. And I wouldn't turn one away. But money and material things cannot motivate creativity. They kill it.

As much as I would like to believe that money could buy happiness. It can't. It buys fun and temporary distractions. Never happiness, no matter how much money you have.

Tom Shadyac is a film director who made a lot of money. I imagine that you've viewed at least one of his movies. He directed *Ace Ventura, The Nutty Professor, Liar Liar,* and *Bruce Almighty*. He amassed a multimillion dollar bank account from the work that he created, and he lived as most of us only dream of living.

Then Tom got into a serious bicycling accident which left him with severe post-concussion symptoms that had him pondering his desire to live.

Fortunately, he made the right choice, to stay alive. That's *always* the right choice. It was during this time of rebirth that he really questioned the reality that has been created for him and for us and came to the conclusion that it was all a lie.

Tom was standing in his posh mansion, stocked with everything he ever wanted, when he realized that he wasn't happier with it than he was before becoming wealthy and collecting all of his material treasures. So he sold it all and moved to a trailer park. Tom wanted to find happiness and then share it with the world. If it wasn't in Beverley Hills, maybe a trailer park was a good place to start his search.

He decided to document his search for happiness in a movie titled *I Am*. It was during the time spent creating this film that he made a very profound discovery. Here it is.

"If you don't do what your heart wants you to do and follow your passion, it will destroy you." Those are Tom's words, not mine. All credit is due to him. But they apply to each and every one of us, not just disenfranchised film directors.

So, happiness is all about passion. So, what was Tom's? He found that his passion was giving. Once he realized this, Tom made it a point to do it as much as possible. He gave it all away, and then he kept on giving. Every single person he encountered took a piece of Tom Shadyac away with them. I'm not talking about part's of his fortune. That will eventually run dry. The pieces of Tom that others continue to take away are parts of what makes Tom Shadyac happy. That is Tom's passion.

What's yours?

Do that as much as possible.

Create Your Own Motivation

Happiness is the supreme motivator. We know that things like money and prestige motivate, but only for a short time. They never, ever move people. Besides, they only motivate action, not creativity or passion. The best ideas are never generated because of money alone. It might have started out with the desire to make money, but somewhere along the way, the motivation changed and the ideas became real passion.

We need to create opportunities for happiness and fun to motivate us throughout all phases of our creative pursuits. From planning, to starting, to enduring the creative plateau, and through shipping, without happiness and fun as a motivator, our aspirations are doomed from the beginning. Our ideas will never connect with people, which is really just a big waste of time, resources, and energy. I call this wishful thinking.

You can find this at Google. Not wishful thinking but happiness throughout the pursuit of their creative ideas.

This was key for Larry Page and Sergey Brin when they created Google, as a research project, in 1996. Since then, Google has moved from its original dorm room to its headquarters at the Googleplex in Mountain View, California.

The work culture at the Googleplex is a bit odd. Or is ours odd and theirs normal? Either way you look at it, Google understands that the greatest motivator in life is happiness. That's why they allow employees to bring their pets to work with them.

That's why they provide free chef-prepared lunches from an array of different cultures.

That's why they have a commuter shuttle bus with Wi-Fi that will pick you up and take you home daily.

That's why they provide all of their employees with an earthquake readiness backpack.

And on any given day, that's why you can take a break from work and go listen to a presentation given by other creatives visiting campus; politicians, professors, authors, environmentalists, journalists, monks, dignitaries, Nobel Prize winners, venture capitalists and more.

If that's not for you, then you can go outside and play sand volleyball instead. Totally your choice.

Google understands that people are not moved by money. We are not inspired by threats or ultimatums.

We are moved by being happy. We're happy when we are in control of ourselves and our time. We're happy when we can be trusted to decide when we work and how we do our work. We're happy when we get to be us.

My favorite aspect of Google's working culture is 20 percent time. In a nutshell, Google engineers are expected to use 20 percent of their contracted time to work on anything company-related that would interest them personally. There are really no other guidelines than that.

Take some time to do what you love that could possibly help the company, and then share it with us. That's basically what 20 percent time is.

It's not a revolutionary discovery, but Google understands that people work better when they are engaged in something they are passionate about doing. That's going to be different for every single person, but it doesn't mean that every single person works alone. They connect.

Some of the new products that have resulted from 20 percent time include Gmail, Google News, and the shuttle bus that I mentioned earlier.

Employees at Google work hard. They play hard as well. Synergistically, they do both together.

As of this writing, Google was on the CNN Money Top 100 Companies to Work For list. They were number 1.

That makes me happy.

Create Happiness for Others

Occasionally, it's not our happiness that motivates us. Sometimes, helping others to be happy is reason enough for us to start moving.

But what do you do when the others that you are trying to help are invisible?

You use your art to shine a light on them.

Jason Russell, Bobby Bailey, and Laren Poole did just that after traveling from the United States to Uganda, Africa.

Only college students at the time, these three boys
shined a light on the children of Uganda. These were
children who were not just afraid of the dark, they were
terrified of it.

Each night, children in Uganda flee in large groups as
the sun goes down. That's when the rebel soldiers of
The Lord's Resistance Army come after them. The rebels
ransack the homes of northern Uganda and rip children
away from their families in mass kidnappings. They
force these youths to become part of The Lord's
Resistance.

If any child refuses to join, he or she is brutally beaten,
tortured, or killed in front of his or her family. Those
who do join are often forced to torture their own kin
and commit grievous acts of violence themselves. This is
a lose/lose situation. It's one that no one should ever
have to experience.

Thankfully, many get away. Those children who do
escape these nightly atrocities go to safe villages to

sleep in hospital basements and bus parks. They are safer there. Every morning, when the refugee children wake up they trek back to their parents and their village to go to school while the sun is still out.

Jason, Bobby, and Laren caught all of this sad reality on film. They were sure to record children sharing their horrifying first-hand stories of life in hiding from The Lord's Resistance Army. The boys called these runaways *Nightwalkers*. And they recorded them so that they could tell their story in a documentary titled *Invisible Children*.

With their message in hand and backed by the thrust of passion, these three filmmakers traveled the United States to tell a story that no one here had yet heard.

Through their efforts, they eventually got the attention of Oprah. It helps that they showed up to her studio with a few hundred really loud people. You can imagine how quickly *Invisible Children* spread after that.

Yet, their aim was not fame. It was not notoriety or launching a career as documentarians. The goal from the moment they the encountered the Nightwalkers was to shine a light on their terrifying situation. So they did.

After the movie was released, Jason, Bobby, and Laren started an organization which they also named Invisible Children. To date, they have raised over $33 million to go toward the cause of ending civil war in Uganda and giving childhood back to those who are too afraid to be children.

All three of these men believe that this will happen very soon. Acting on their idea helps.

Happiness Matters

It matters more than we can ever imagine. Where happiness to us might mean a three-day weekend or bigger toys, happiness to others means being able to go to sleep in the same place as their parents.

Happiness has driven the global movement that is *Invisible Children*. Happiness can drive you. If you let it, it will.

If three college students on an adventure can overcome a violent guerilla army to pursue happiness for others, surely you can overcome the fear and uncertainty that stands between happiness and you.

The cost of inaction far outweighed the price tag on time, energy, and resources to do something and create *Invisible Children.*

The first step to success was simple.

Starting.

Without starting, your ideas are simply wishful thinking. That's never made anyone happy.

A Premium On Starting

We have plenty of critics. It seems like almost everyone is at the ready to criticize the world. What we need more of are people who are willing to redesign it.

They're not going to be corporations, human rights groups, and religions alone. The greatest redesign will come from us. It will come from what we have. It will come from what we do. And it will come from where we go.

We just need to stir up the chutzpah to get going; going anywhere. Yes, the world is full of critics, but the loudest one is me. It's you. Ironically, we are almost always wrong about the judgments we pass on our own ideas, yet our targeted shame is the loudest and hardest to ignore.

We will never be perfect no matter how hard we try to convince ourselves that we need to be. Quite opposite of that, we will always be vulnerable and imperfect. We are flawed creatures, and that's okay. I tend to think that some of the best ideas are those with unique imperfections. They add character and verify that it was dreamt up by a human.

As with visual art, you can find iterations of masterpieces for quite cheap. They're everywhere, and they're perfectly produced for us to have. But are they ultimately as valuable as the originals? Or do we value them because they are conveniently placed where we can easily find them? We are challenged by the hunt for true art. It's out of the way, indiscrete, without a package, and dark. Since each of us were children we've been afraid of the dark.

Do we really know what's in there? Have you gone yet? Or do we just listen to rumors of what others have heard is beyond the threshold of light?

In the depths of darkness you will find success. You will also find failure. The dark is uncertainty, and there is a premium on those who are willing to venture into the darkness. While we set out to create successful art, often times we don't want to experience failure along the way. This ruins any chance of it being truly successful.

Here's the irony. While success is found only in the depths of the unknown, failure is not constrained to this black hole. It is emitted like radiation from the real thing. It's all around us, and the only way to escape it is to go.

We really have no other options for long term success. We cannot make art in our comfort zones. We need to face our fears and go into dark places. Once there, we will see what we were truly afraid of.

It's that our ideas really can work.

Life is Good

I know a guy who has really great ideas for new business concepts. He is able to connect a need to an audience along with a location. Weekly, he wows me with his knack for problem solving.

But he's never acted on any of his ideas.

There have been a few times where he has talked about his ideas for so long without actually starting that someone else has sneaked in and did what my friend only talks about, and they do it to great success. Now he talks about how he had the idea first. And it matters to no one.

We only care about starting.

You might start a new concept for a building design, a blog, a new gourmet dish, or a book that you've always wanted to write. The Jacobs brothers started a new concept for designing T-shirts.

They knew nothing about the business, but they had the idea to start. Going door to door on college campuses in residence halls hawking their merchandise was how they marketed their idea. As you can imagine, there wasn't much success to be had among the poor college crowd. The designs they were selling weren't that remarkable either. That's when the Jacobs brothers met Jake.

Jake isn't a person. He's a doodle that one of the brothers had sketched. He's a smiley face with an ethos, *Life is good*. And he was hanging up on a bedroom wall.

Life is good. That's sexy and provocative in its simplicity. It's entirely refreshing in a landscape where we are bombarded by messages that life is in no way good.

With a better idea than they had started with, Bert and John Jacobs printed up 48 shirts with Jake's contagious grin and novel reminder for everyone to see. Their plan was to try to sell as many as they could at an upcoming street fair in Cambridge, Massachusetts. Hopefully, this idea would pull through.

They set up shop on the side of the street with 48 shirts and a rickety card table. Oh yeah, and Jake. If only they could sell enough to break even by the end of the day, that would be a huge success.

That didn't happen for the Jacobs brothers. Not even close.

They sold completely out of their inventory *by lunchtime*. Jake had launched, and what would become Life is Good, the company, started on the side of a street fair one fateful day in September when the Jacobs brothers decided to start.

If you've never bought a Jake shirt, you should. Life is Good spreads optimism with every single product they ship, which by now is a lot. Currently, Jake and Life is Good merchandise are sold in over 4,500 retailers in the U.S., online, and in 30 countries around the world. None of them use rickety card tables either.

Needless to say, Jake is pretty big. So are ideas fueled by optimism.

Head of the School

"Everybody is a genius. But if you judge a fish by its ability to climb a tree, it will live its whole life believing it is stupid."

Albert Einstein said that. He wasn't actually talking about fish though. He was talking about you and me. We like to judge everyone by the same criteria without consideration for their relative place in this world.

Fish are remarkable swimmers. They are incredibly social creatures as well. Science has discovered that schools of fish behave quite similarly to groups of humans in a democratic society. People who study fish have observed how schools of fish form and start moving together collectively. Oddly, they do so with only 5 percent of the group leading the way.

Sound familiar?

The super majority of fish in a school, 95 percent, congregate and start migrating in the same direction as 5 percent of their community. Why?

This might lead you to believe that among fish there are some naturally spawned leaders. Unfortunately, this isn't the case. As it is with humans, there are simply too many who are afraid to lead and blindly follow someone else instead.

In other words, the 95% that are followers have no idea where they are going, and the 5% that lead have all of the freedom and control.

The minority that we follow says that the way to succeed is to work hard at your job, to get all As, save money, make your bed, and plan for the future. In fact, we're led to believe that this applies to every single one of us. Doesn't that sound like judging a fish for his ability to climb a tree?

This mentality is standardized. It doesn't care about us personally. It refers to 100% of the group doing the exact same thing while 95% of the members never ask why.

I've never met anyone who has followed their passion by waking up every day to go work for someone else, learn for someone else, or save for someone else. No one wants to make someone else's art.

That's an old model of living. It's a remnant of the Industrial Age, an age that we do not live in anymore. We live in an idea economy where ideas matter and new ones are in high demand. They are free to those willing to dream them up. That's you and me.

Do we realize that? Or are we just part of the school, swimming wherever the person in front of us goes?

It's Here When You're Ready to Start

Few people are comfortable acknowledging that the world that we live in has changed. It is an uncomfortable thing to do. Admitting that is even more disconcerting if we know that we have not changed with it. It's like admitting that the clothes you wear are out of style. It would require us to admit that we need to change as well.

If you talk to my grandfather, or probably yours, he will tell you that the secret to success is working harder than anyone else. If you work hard and mind your manners, you will eventually work yourself into prosperity.

That worked for him. He worked a farm. If you do too, then you might just want to continue outworking the rest of the crowd. That's the way to sell your yield.

Most of us don't grow wheat or potatoes. Instead, we grow ideas. That's what people want more than anything else on the market right now. They want you.

Pursuing successful ideas isn't about working for the longest amount of time. Ideas do not succeed in proportion to the amount of hours you spend working on them. A new secret of the age that we have moved into is working smarter.

We live in the Age of Connections where ideas are our currency. Any type of resource, tool, person, or expertise that we could possibly need is no more than a few clicks away. And the information that I'm searching for is equidistant from my reach in America as it is from a computer user in Bangladesh.

If you want to write for an audience, you start a free blog.

If you want to tell jokes in your own stand-up comedy act, you create a podcast.

If you want to start a band and book gigs across the country, you market yourself on MySpace Music or Reverb Nation.

If you want to host your own art gallery, you do it on Instagram or Flickr.

If you want to launch your independent film career, you upload your productions to YouTube.

Everything that I just mentioned, and more, is free for us to use. We no longer have to bury our best ideas because we don't own the means of production. In our Age of Connections, we are the means of production. In an idea economy, we are the ones creating the currency. We don't produce recyclable goods or gizmos with interchangeable parts.

We make ideas that matter. There's no assembly line for that. But often, it helps to connect with the right people.

Twitter and a Modern Day Pharaoh

"Insomniac, I twitter away, mournful as a sparrow in the gutter." That is from Psalms 102:7. If you're on Twitter, you've most likely had this biblical experience.

A micro-blogging social-network, Twitter has connected people, companies, and ideas like nothing has ever done before. And it has done it in the shortest time possible.

Conceived during a brainstorm session by three workers at IDEO, the idea of an individual being able to send SMS messages to a small group between phones took flight.

The definition of the word *twitter* means a short burst of inconsequential information. At the time Jack Dorsey, Biz Stone, and Evan Williams connected to come up with the idea for Twitter they thought the name fit perfectly.

That's why hindsight is so nice to have. I imagine the three developers would say that what is happening on Twitter now is anything but inconsequential.

Where Johannes Gutenberg empowered the world with the ability to access text-based information, Twitter has empowered the world to access each other, along with our ideas, wisdoms, and our talents.

Now, if you want to get a message to the President, you don't have to find his contact information. You Tweet him.

If you want to connect with people in your field or people who share the same interests as you, you can do that on a global scale during breakfast.

I saw what Twitter had to offer and signed up for my account in 2012.

Egypt saw it sooner.

In 2011, Egyptians decided that they wanted change. Their president, Hosni Mubarak, had been in power for 30 years and had let the people down to say the least.

In one of the first large-scale acts of social protest through social networking sites, the people of Egypt started telling their story over Twitter. What they had to say was raw, provocative, and telling.

The Egyptian government recognized the power of Twitter in this grassroots movement. So they did what they could to protect themselves. They deactivated many of the country's cell phone towers, stifling reception and the ability to Tweet.

Twitter confirmed this with a Tweet of their own on the day that Egypt fell offline. The company sent out a Tweet verifying that Egypt had indeed blocked Twitter. The Tweet went on to reaffirm that Twitter enables an open exchange of information and views, which ideally *should* connect a government with their people.

The Egyptian government didn't see it this way. Unfortunately for the Egyptian government, their citizens did.

The uprising began January 11. The regime came down on February 25. Hosni Mubarak, once referred to as a modern pharaoh, was sentenced to life in prison for being an accessory in murder after failing to stop the killing of unarmed civilians during the uprising. With a massive platform for their voices to be heard, Egyptians brought down their government in less than two months. No, the revolution would not be televised. It would be Tweeted.

I don't know if this could have happened with e-mail alone. It didn't have to. We live in a world where everything we need in order for us to achieve what we set our minds to is sitting around waiting for us to use it.

Seth Godin said it this way, "Freedom isn't the ability to do whatever you want, it's the willingness to do whatever you want."

Passion Is Not In Short Supply: It's Just Not Tapped Into

Everyone has something that drives them. We all have something that our minds turn to when we find that our minds are being wasted with what we are doing. J.K. Rowling stripped away the inessential to focus on finishing the only work that mattered to her. Her passion is for writing.

Tony Hsieh told his parents that he didn't want to go to medical or law school. He wanted to sell shoes. His passion is for connecting with the customer.

I could fill the rest of this book with a list of people and what their passions are, but that would be procrastinating. You're not wondering what others are passionate about.

You're wondering what your passion is.

I don't know what you are passionate about. But you do.

It might have simply been buried or stifled by being told that following your passion isn't practical or promising. Creatives are marginalized by those who are too reluctant to be creative themselves.

Perhaps it was okay for you to dream when you were a child, but once you got into high school you were told to start focusing on what you *really* wanted to do with your life.

Somehow, that turned into you doing what someone else doesn't want to do for themselves. That's not art. That's not anything. It's inauthentic, and the world is full of that.

It's time to shake things up. It's time to be yourself. If you have something that burns inside you, it's time to let it out and to stick it in front of everyone else's noses.

Banksy

I've never been to Disneyland. If you have, I would expect you to have vivid memories of your favorite rides and attractions. It might be the Matterhorn, Space Mountain, or the Tower of Terror. Each of these rides has an element of the unexpected.

Do you remember anything about the Rocky Mountain Railroad Ride?

If you happened to get a seat on this ride during 2006, you might remember the Guantanamo Bay inmate standing shackled just inside the attraction. Or, you might have missed him.

He was there for just over an hour before Disneyland workers noticed him, shut down the ride, and removed this work of art.

You read that right. The hooded figure in the orange jumpsuit with hands and feet shackled was a statement. Surely, it wasn't put there by anyone from the Magical Kingdom. It had patrons scratching their heads. In such a high-traffic place, how did something so sneaky happen there?

It happened the same way that the elephant's thoughts were graffiti painted on a wall inside of its pen at the London Zoo.

I want out. This place is too cold. Keeper smells. Boring, boring, boring.

And the exact same way that controversial paintings were surreptitiously hung in the Museum of Modern Art, the Metropolitan Museum of Art, the Brooklyn Museum, and the American Museum of Natural History.

One word. Banksy.

A self-dubbed guerilla artist, little is really known about the man who painted what looked like a gaping hole having been taken out of the West Bank Wall in Israel, the walled border that makes Palestine essentially the world's largest prison. Through the hole, a relaxing tropical beach appeared. While very realistic looking, it was all just paint. And Banksy painted it.

The art that Banksy creates around the world is much more than just paint, however. It moves people. It's social commentary. It makes us think. It's passion. Banksy's art is a story that he has created to tell. It was an idea that was started. And most importantly, it is his own.

Get Out of the Drive-Thru

We can go to McDonald's, order our mediocre food into a microphone, and be told to pull up to the second window. That's how McDonald's thrives. Real life doesn't tell us where to go to get what we want. We can't just follow the drive-thru lane to a full sense of being.

In the same vein, life is not going to come around to pick us. No one at McDonald's, anywhere in the world, is going to walk around town asking you if you would like a Happy Meal. The same goes for the value that you have to spread with your art.

To live authentically, we need to choose what we want for ourselves and then get it. We need to write and live our own stories instead of role-playing someone else's narrative. We need to bring the audience to us instead of waiting to be invited to perform for them.

Banksy does this. So do flash mobs.

First organized by Bill Wasik, then a magazine editor for *Harper's Magazine*, a flash mob is a social experiment designed to temporarily take over a commercial or public place by a sudden assembly of people just to show you that they can.

Wasik's first flash mob was on the ninth floor of Macy's in Manhattan in 2003. Having been organized over email, more than 130 people showed up in the rug department and gathered around a very expensive rug. Once they did, everyone just stood there.

The congregation had been given specific instructions, particularly for when a store employee approached them about what was going on. They were advised to tell any sales assistant that the group lived in a warehouse on the fringe of New York. They were there to buy a "love rug", but they had to make all of their decisions in a group.

That was it.

130 people or so got together and stared at a rug. The point was not to harass or embarrass anyone at Macy's. It was to make a point. The very first flash mob was

designed to lampoon New York hipsters telling others what the next big thing was going to be.

If even for only ten minutes, Bill Wasik made the next big thing an overpriced rug.

For then, at least, it was.

You Are the Next Big Thing

if you want to be.

Emotional Labor

One of my favorite people once said,

As human beings, our job in life is to help people realize how rare and valuable each one of us really is, that each of us has something that no one else has—or ever will have—something inside that is unique to all time. It's our job to encourage each other to discover that

uniqueness and to provide ways of developing its
expression.

His name was Mister Rogers.

Mister Rogers, or Fred as his family knew him, was
definitely unique. He was an advocate for children.
Through his television show, *Mister Rogers'*
Neighborhood, Fred Rogers spoke to the fears that most
children experience, fears that we've all had.

Whether divorce, death, the first day of school, or being
sucked down the bathtub drain, Fred Rogers
understood, and he had a way of helping everyone else
understand what they were feeling too. I remember
watching episodes of *Mister Rogers' Neighborhood* on
PBS every single weekday as a child. I was caught up by
the way that he spoke as if he was speaking directly to
me.

Even now, I still think of Mister Rogers as someone who
seemed to know me and provided a connection to me

as I grew up with the insecurities and fears reserved for an only child in a single-parent home.

It wasn't just me that Fred reached. Before and after I watched his show, Mister Rogers was connecting with purpose.

He started the first version of what would become the nationally recognized *Mister Rogers' Neighborhood* in Canada in 1961. That was two years before either of my parents were even born. For over 40 years, Mister Rogers would take boys and girls, young and old to The Land of Make Believe where they didn't have to be afraid of anything.

His was a labor of love. It was what psychology has come to label emotional labor. Emotional labor is when the work that you do is not to simply create a new model or product, but a new feeling inside of another human being. This is the most important work we can do. Your ideas should do this.

It's not hard to figure out either. We are surrounded by people in our lives who affect us emotionally whether we recognize it or not. Naturally, the work of some is more obvious than the work of others.

Fred's work was great, and it continues to scale. That's where manual labor and emotional labor diverge. You can only work so hard, or so fast, or so long before there is nothing left for you to possibly give. That's when manual labor stops. The hole is dug. The day is over. The tank is out of gas.

Emotional labor is not like this. It continues working long after our emotional acts of service is over. It grows and spreads like the dark matter of our universe. There's no telling where it will actually stop.

The idea that fuels your passion will surely require manual labor. Whether constructing, writing, digging, driving, cutting, painting, drafting, or designing, there is work to be done. Manual labor is not to be disregarded. It's simply that it is no longer the vehicle to success in the world we inhabit. And often, you can get someone else to do it for you.

The emotional labor of connecting with human beings is what is really in demand now. It's so highly sought after because the supply of those willing to face the possibilities of their passions is short. The courage to share your ideas with someone else is even more scarce. Passion involves risk and a very real chance of failure along the way. Sharing it makes us vulnerable. Others don't think like we do. They might not like it, and reject it.

We've been programmed to associate failure with being a loser. Failing, we are told, is incapability. It's falling short. It's embarrassing. Therefore, failure should be avoided.

I don't buy that, and neither should you. The sting of failure is a lot more painful than the sting of thinking that you cannot make a difference. You might call that regret. However you view it, it's short-lived. It will end.

Life will continue if you let it. You won't hurt for long. On the other hand, how long have you been led to believe that your ideas don't actually matter?

That really hurts.

How Does Your Art Care About Other People?

If it doesn't add value to your life, don't do it. If it can possibly add value to the life of another, you don't have the option of keeping it to yourself. You must take action to deliver your ideas.

No one on the face of the Earth could have possibly done what Mister Rogers did quite like Fred did it himself. That's because it was his own unique idea. It was driven by passion. That passion was about adding value to the lives of as many children and grown-ups as possible. It was about helping them to overcome fear and see the world for what it really is.

Fred did that.

Now it is your turn. What value are you creating? That is your art. You must share it.

Make a connection between your idea and someone else. That someone else is growing exponentially larger every day. We're no longer isolated to our own communities, where the only possible connections are with our neighbors and mailmen. We've been given permission to connect with the world.

We know that emotional labor scales. So do connections; often quicker than you would expect.

1 Million Connections

The Cordell family had to say goodbye to their family pet after their dog lost his battle with cancer. A mother, a father, and their five children mourned the loss of a family member just as anyone else would do.

With time, the hurting became manageable, and the children wanted the joy of having a dog in their family again. Understandably so, their dad did not want to endure that type of loss a second time, and he was not so willing to let his children persuade him otherwise.

As I'm sure you already know, children are very tenacious. Ryan Cordell, the patriarch of the family, knew this too. Eventually, he stopped saying no. Instead, Mr. Cordell decided to let his determined children come to "no" as the answer themselves.

Dad created a Facebook page, which he monitored, for his kids, and he made them an offer they could not refuse. If they could get 1 million people to "Like" a photo of them asking for a dog on the social networking platform, then he would agree to get his children a puppy.

So, the five Cordell children created a poster. With colored markers on a white paper canvas they scrawled their call to action.

Hi World. We want a puppy! Our dad said we could get one if we get 1 million likes. He doesn't think we can do it! So like this!

They had a picture taken of them holding up the sign in their living room and had dad post it on their Facebook page.

Having seemingly won the battle, Ryan Cordell tucked his hopeful children into bed. He'd no longer have to say no. His kids would fail and realize that a puppy just wasn't happening. Availed, he, too, went to bed.

As dawn broke and Ryan Cordell woke up, he checked the page to see if any of his family or friends had clicked "Like" on the photo. Some of them had. Under the picture that he had taken of his children, roughly twelve hours earlier, he saw how many "Likes" their wishful thinking had received.

1,000,000 "Likes" slapped him in the face with an endless comment thread to prove it.

It was just a picture of his kids with a sign. They didn't even know 1 million people to begin with. Even so, Ryan had made an agreement with his kids, and the conditions were met.

That morning the family went to a local shelter to get a puppy.

Two Girls and a Puppy, the name of the Cordell's Facebook page, succeeded to connect over 1 million people because of three aspects of their campaign. It was not because of fame. It had nothing to do with wealth. The Cordell's didn't know any mainstream taste makers either.

Their message was simple. Their call to action was doable. But the most important element was that their idea was based on a good cause. It was valuable to the Cordell's, to their new puppy, and to over 1 million strangers on Facebook.

Was there really a good enough reason to *not* click "Like"?

Value Spreads

How? By tipping. Malcolm Gladwell wrote an entire book about this. *The Tipping Point* explains change and how new ideas can spread quickly and quite often unexpectedly. I recommend reading Gladwell's work. You won't be disappointed.

So, how do ideas tip?

Connections. Are you surprised?

We need to connect our ideas with the market. Who's yours? In a world that has become open to anyone willing to roam around, your market might be larger than you think. It's no longer any more difficult to connect with someone in Budapest than it is in Boise, Idaho.

But the first connection must be with you. Does your idea resonate with your values? Is it something that you are passionate about because it taps into your innate being? Or are you doing it for the money?

Back at Google, Larry Page sells happiness. It is part of who Larry is.

But you're not Larry Page. You are you. Once you can figure out how to connect your passion with your work, then you will be able to connect your work with your intended audience, your market. Then your market will connect it with theirs. Theirs with theirs. And then . . .

it tips.

It's all about targeting the right market.

Lehman's

In 1955, the world was being introduced to TV. Elvis Presley was rock and roll. Americans wanted baseboard heating and huge automobiles. And in a town called Kidron, somewhere in Ohio, Jay Lehman decided to start selling tools that no one made anymore.

Kidron is in Amish country. Jay Lehman loves the Amish culture. Afraid that someday soon his neighbors would not be able to continue on with their simple way of living, Jay opened a non-electric hardware store in a pre-Civil War building. He named it Lehman's.

Wanting to preserve the past for future generations, Lehman's started crafting, stocking, and selling items including butter churns, apple peelers, drying racks, and washboards. Obviously, Lehman's wouldn't appeal to everyone. But Jay Lehman didn't want to.

He wanted to serve a market niche. So that's exactly what he did.

He made everything Lehman's sold, and he made each item to snuff. The community was grateful, and Jay loved what he did.

Eventually, word got out about Lehman's. People far outside of their little Kidron community started talking about the non-electric hardware store. Now Lehman's sells to those people too. Those people just happen to live all across the world. They're missionaries, hunters, cabin dwellers, and the nostalgic. Some of those people are even big time movie set designers who want historically accurate pieces.

Lehman's sells to all of them. But it makes its products for the Amish in Kidron. That is its market niche. That's why it is Lehman's.

Why Bon Jovi Hates Steve Jobs So Much

I once read an interview where Jon Bon Jovi claimed that Steve Jobs killed the record store. He was referring to the advent of iTunes empowering people to sample an entire album before buying what they wanted.

It used to be that you would go to your local music shop to buy a new album knowing only the songs that you heard on the radio and what the album's jacket looked like. To Bon Jovi, this was a magical experience.

So, did Steve Jobs kill the record store?

No.

He took down the entire music industry.

In 2003, the first year that the iTunes software was available to the public, 30 million digital downloads of music were sold. After two years, that 30 million downloads turned into 2.1 billion. With unprecedented access to all types of music, iTunes connected us with our favorite musicians and bands.

It was a sad day for the record shop. The industry had just had the rug pulled out from under them. Bon Jovi might have been the only one attending the record store's funeral. It looks as if everyone else was too busy buying music on iTunes.

Jobs' new music software changed the way that we sampled, bought, and shared music. It brought more music into our homes than any record store could ever dream of stocking. Through its different versions, iTunes has connected us with what other listeners with a similar taste in music are listening to and buying.

It suggests artists and groups that we might have never heard of, but would possibly like. And iTunes has created a way for anyone with a passion for making music to share their idea with the music world. Artists weren't left hoping to be discovered by an agent or a record label anymore. They *were* the record label, and iTunes was their record shop.

You no longer have to live in New York City or Los Angeles to fuel a successful music career. You can launch it from your laptop.

And people listen.

Well, maybe not Bon Jovi.

Conflict Welcomed

Jobs caused waves. He welcomed conflict. It reaffirmed that what he was doing was remarkable and new. If no one is willing to remark on your work, then who is going to hear about it? Who is going to care?

We tend to surround ourselves with the cushion of conventional wisdom. If it's been done before and worked, then we might as well keep doing what's working. Right?

Wrong.

No one talks about what has been working. They talk about things that work better.

Conventional wisdom is untested. It's accepted by large groups and experts in their fields because it is convenient. Good ideas are convenient.

Remarkable ideas are something totally different. Nothing about them is conventional. And people talk about them a lot.

Can I Rent Your Igloo?

Somewhere in between staying in a hotel and couch surfing at a friend's house, you'll find Airbnb. Originally named Airbed and Breakfast, the concept of renting out your extra spaces has exploded for this online company.

Started by two roommates in San Francisco, Airbnb was a solution to insufficient rent funds. Brian Chesky and Joe Gebbia needed money, so they inflated an air mattress, plopped it down in their living room, and told anyone willing to rent it that they would provide breakfast for them in the morning.

Now, six years after the idea was launched, Airbnb has gone international and booked over 5 million accommodations. It's not just the guys' air mattress anymore. It's really not even just air mattresses.

Ranging from spare bedrooms to guest houses and tipis to igloos, Airbnb has its own website that allows users to list their space in a searchable public forum, no VIP card needed.

People looking to skip the expensive short-term hotel stays can connect with a trusted Airbnb host for some rest and relaxation while networking with real authentic people. You might not get a mint on your pillow by booking through Airbnb, but travelers who use Airbnb are looking for more. A lot more. And they've found it.

I searched Airbnb's website to see if there was anyone around where I live that hosted through the company, and I was surprised to see that someone down the street was successfully renting out a tent in their backyard.

We live in between Salt Lake City and Yellowstone. Their tent offering was a perfect stop for those travelling either way along Interstate-15. And those who have stayed there absolutely loved the experience.

I can tell you that with confidence because Airbnb empowers their users to post feedback and suggestions on their site directly under specific listings.

With this location near my home, I was able to see a photo of the host family (it's a young husband and wife with two infant sons), their contact information (they encourage texting or calling anytime for information), their rules for visitors (which include no loud partying or drug use), and a picture of what they provide along with their backyard tent (access to a fire pit, chopped wood, and hot dog roasters).

Most powerful for me were the comments from those who have stayed at this location before. Entirely positive, visitors shared their stories of what brought them to this suburban backyard. They were pleased with being able to camp out in a tent that was already set up for them along with an inflated air mattress, bedding, accessories, and a portable ice box.

What made the experience so enjoyable for the eclectic crowd of travelers was the connection and hospitality they received from the host family. This particular family allowed visitors to use their indoor facilities as needed. They also invited them in to visit and socialize as desired.

The family down my street understands the value of connections. Theirs were literally sitting in their own backyard.

Those who stayed left saying that they would be back the next time they passed through town, a testament to the worthwhile adventure and good time.

While hotel chains compete for customers by price and accommodation, a new alternative has arisen providing much more value than simply access to a community pool. An idea that generated from a genuine problem is transforming the world space by space through connecting real people to real places.

Brian Chesky and Joe Gebbia didn't scale their accidental company just because they saw a good idea. They saw something they could get obsessed about. It drove their passions. As with anything we do, passion fuels the engine. It's quite remarkable, isn't it.

And It's often found in the most unusual places.

Khan

When I think of conventional wisdom, I think of school. If one relic remains to remind us of the Industrial Age, look no further than the classroom. The fear of change is ubiquitous in the American education system. Instead of changing the way kids are taught, we change the way they are monitored. We track them in tiers and treat them accordingly. If all works out as planned, there will be no dings or scratches on the finished product. At least, that's what the experts say.

Perhaps this is why a girl named Nadia went to her older cousin for help understanding math instead of her dispassionate teacher. Nadia's cousin, Sal, used Yahoo's Doodle Pad to teach her math online. He recorded his lessons while writing the formulas and explanations on his home computer for Nadia to view from where she lived.

When more friends and family heard about this, they called on Sal to help them as well. Seeing a better way to reach those who needed him, Sal started putting these recorded videos on YouTube so that anyone could view them.

Unforeseen to Cousin Sal, anyone did view them. In fact, *everyone* watched what he had recorded, and they left their appreciative feedback on the YouTube comments thread for him to see. When Sal Khan saw them, he quit his job.

He was a hedge fund analyst, but decided that he wanted to start devoting himself to creating a collection of open online courses like the ones that he was informally creating for his cousin Nadia instead. Uncle Sal had a vision, and he started.

Thus, Khan Academy was born.

Before Khan Academy, Sal Khan graduated with three degrees from MIT, coincidentally one of the forerunners in the open online-course movement that Sal had just become a part of. Ironically, Khan's open courses have now eclipsed the popularity and traffic of MIT's free online offerings by roughly 160 million views as of this writing.

Khan Academy doesn't just teach math. Since its genesis, Khan's not-for-profit company has created courses in all areas of science, history, economics, art, finance, computer science, and grammar, just to name a small sampling of subjects.

Students can view videos at their own pace, essentially having the capability of pausing and rewinding their teacher. Who couldn't benefit from doing that?

Khan Academy has also designed self-assessment and self-pacing features that puts the control over progress and mastery in the hands of each learner.

Leveraging the ability to teach many people is one aspect of this project that caught Bill Gates' eye and inspired him to support Khan Academy with financial donations. Google has jumped in too along with a multitude of other financiers which have allowed Sal Khan to hire a full-time staff to help him as they create their online content and translate it into as many different languages as possible.

Traditional educators are in a tizzy. They've started flooding Sal's YouTube comment threads with cynical comments and criticism. Perhaps that's because they see what Sal is doing and it forces them to look beyond their comfort zone. There's finally someone willing to buck conventional wisdom for a model that works. Now, I'm no expert, but it is working.

Get Used to Starting

The easiest part of idea generation is coming up with an idea. Each of us already do this daily. The hardest part is actually doing something about it. We don't do that enough.

Those ideas that intersect with a market aren't necessarily even the best of their kind. Today, in our idea economy, they don't need to be. They just need to be acted on. The best idea is worthless if nobody knows about it. That's why the one that is projected into the market is better than the best.

Once you have an idea that you want to pursue, stop thinking about it, and take the first actionable step to launch your big idea.

You will experience mistakes along the way. I think I have beaten that point to a lifeless pulp. But the biggest mistake that you could potentially experience is not starting. Nothing of value comes from that. You could potentially create negative value for yourself by not launching though.

With the stories and experiences that I have recounted here, you might believe that a good idea, one worth acting on, has to be grandiose and lifestyle altering. Some are. Most aren't. Yours by no means has to be. It just has *to be*.

Create a new code. Propose a project. Open an Etsy or eBay online store. Grab your laptop and start typing. Paint your living room. Record your first video and publish it on a YouTube channel. Whatever idea you've been keeping to yourself. Now is the time to share it with the world. Put down this book and start something right now. Now is conveniently the best time to start.

What luck!

Become More Self-Aware

The lizard brain is still there. It always will be. The idea is not to eliminate it. It is to manage it. We do that by understanding what it is and where it comes from. The panacea for the fear of failing is this, know yourself.

The most successful creators know that the Lizard exists and is a part of who they are. They don't let fear control them. Instead, they control their biological reactions to fear. They stop reacting to their lizard brains and start responding. Reacting is impulsive. We react when someone jumps out at us from behind a wall.

Responding is intentional. We respond when we process information and make educated choices for ourselves.

The more self-aware we become, the more we will respond. The more we respond, the greater tolerance for uncertainty we will have. Uncertainty is where we should all be headed.

Let's start with this. What are you ultimately afraid of happening when you act on your passion? Literally write each of these things down on a piece of paper. It does not matter how little or large they are. List them all to increase your awareness.

Cross out the events or experiences that will last less than one month. You can make it through 30 days of failing.

Now, cross out any that are out of your locus of control. Worrying about these is wasted energy anyway. You are reacting to these problems.

Third, cross out those that are exaggerations. These are easy to spot. They generally start with "well, what if?".

Finally, ask yourself whether what you have left is a practical fear. If it is, take each fear and break it down into small, manageable steps to overcome. That might include sitting your wife down to explain how much this pursuit means to you and persuading her to get on board. It might mean selling a few things online to raise some needed capital. It might even be making a phone call or two today.

Once you have each fear broken down into manageable action steps. Start walking. Go. Respond to each one.

The issue is no longer fear, it's which one are you going to tackle first?

Then Create Another List

Before you get too caught up in what could possibly go wrong, make a second list. On the same sheet of paper write down the potential outcomes of acting on an idea. If it could potentially result from you taking action, make sure it ends up in your list. This one is going to be a lot longer. I promise. In fact, you might need to get some more paper.

Once you're done listing all of the potential positive results, set your pencil down. There's no crossing out needed with this list. There's no dreaming allowed either. Just action.

By the way, which list is longer?

This Idea Should Have Never Worked

Brian Scudamore, the son of a liver transplant surgeon, found himself sitting in traffic behind a truck full of junk. That might rank as one of the best moments of his life.

At the time, only one year away from graduating college, Brian met his big idea. If you were to tell him it was junk. Brian would entirely agree. It was junk that inspired him. His idea was to take other people's unwanted junk off their hands and dispose of it for them. You don't want to do that. I'm sure of it. Have you ever sat in line on a Saturday at the junkyard?

That's exactly why Brian Scudamore did it.

The twenty-something college student wasted no time in going out and buying a truck for $700. He needed something to load other people's cargo in.

Then he started working.

Just a few days after beginning his FedEx of junk removal, Brian hired a friend to help him meet the demand of being a junkman. Clearly, Brian's idea was one that others had been waiting for.

He didn't know anything about hiring, but Brian knew that he didn't want to contract out. In his opinion, hiring communicated his belief in the success of his new business while contracting for short term help said that he didn't expect much to happen over the long run.

So Brian kept hiring. Apparently, offering to pick up other people's trash in a shiny new truck by employees in good looking uniforms was something that customers liked.

They liked it so much that Brian started franchising his company, 1-800-Got Junk. As of this writing, Brian Scudamore's spur-of-the-moment idea has over 200 franchises. It's saved over 1 million pounds of junk from ending up in a landfill. And Brian's initial investment of $700 has grown into a business model worth more than $100 million.

If Brian Scudamore had decided to simply chew the idea over while eating his burger and fries, he would be $100 million poorer than he is today, probably buying his next meal at a drive-thru. Because he responded, he's not. Ironically, he could probably buy the same drive-thru where he connected with his original idea.

What a load.

Your Most Important Asset

When it comes to idea generation, we are playing on a level field. We all have exactly what we need to get started, the holy grail of creativity. We've just been taught to use it incorrectly. When given lemons, we all assume that the best thing to do is make lemonade. There are other uses for lemons, you know.

Blame it on our minds. We're not leveraging it for all that it can do because other people have told us to not do that.

Attribute it to our lizard brains, that sneaky amygdala sitting atop of our brainstem. Work and school has nourished this fear mill to follow the rules. Compliance leads to efficiency, productivity, and low quality production that are just good enough, which is what most people are willing to accept.

Creativity doesn't come from our lizard brains. Being creative is far too risky.

The rub is that the world is made by those who are willing to take risks. They are change agents. And we need them. *We need us*. Creatives are those who are willing to look at a problem as an opportunity. Instead of asking *Is it safe?* they ask *Is it interesting?*

Safe and interesting are discrete.

Don't go drive your car 100 miles per hour down a residential road. That's not safe nor interesting. That's stupid. I'm referring to intellectual safety. Are we taking our thoughts out of the comfort zone that we have been given and seeking out the uncertainty of interesting, or are we accepting what we can learn while being safe? Parenthetically, you can't learn much while being safe.

If our most important asset were capital, we would risk losing some to invest it. If our most important asset were people, we would risk time in a cubicle to enable brainstorming and collaboration. If our most important asset were customer relations, we would risk losing a large portion of income to cut out the middle man.

Our most important asset is our mind, no matter what it is we do. Risk the comfort of certainty to embark on an adventure into the unknown. Like connections and emotional labor, intellectual risk scales.

What do you want to get from it?

The Last Surviving Dodo

Dodo birds are extinct. Evidenced as existing as late as the 17th Century, this flightless bird was not afraid of humans or predators. The species died off as the result of deforestation and hunting. But in San Francisco, one final Dodo still exists and thrives even though everything around it says it shouldn't.

DodoCase is a unique company that you should like. I'll tell you why throughout this account, but the first reason is because they are risky.

On paper, nothing about their business model should have succeeded. They produce their product in one of the most expensive cities to do so in the world. They don't have an office or a central production location. They make everything by hand using antiquated methods and technology which severely slow down production. And they started out making their line of products for an item they had not seen or held when they did so.

DodoCase makes iPad and iPhone covers. But they don't make them like anyone else does. Their covers aren't manufactured in a third-party production warehouse. They are made by local book binders in San Francisco who would have otherwise been out of a job.

Book binding is a dying art. It's a beautiful skill, and I'm sure you would appreciate it if you ever saw it done. Our books are quickly becoming bound by binary code instead of hands. But in the Bay Area, DodoCase still takes time to create a remarkable product that you can only get from them.

They designed the first DodoCase having not yet used an iPad. What they saw was a new technology and a new way to make it better. No need to wait for permission to get to work launching this idea. They took a risk and did it as soon as the idea was had.

Important in their product is ensuring that each new case is unique with a story to tell. San Francisco has a rich book binding community. Like others, it was suffering. So DodoCase made it a point to value them for the specialized skill that book binders have to offer. Each DodoCase ordered is specially handcrafted by a San Franciscan book binder using traditional techniques developed hundreds of years ago.

As they launched their first line of products and started accepting orders, their customers had to wait. The item that was ordered had to be custom made. Patience paid off for the company and the customers though. In a fast-food nation, the time and effort put into the design and creation returned indisputable reviews.

Their anxiously waiting customers absolutely love their DodoCases once they finally hold them in their hands. That's a fact.

On paper, DodoCase was a terrible idea. On paper, it was doomed to fail by all standards. That's why we've got to stop putting our ideas on paper.

Off paper, DodoCase is an idea fueled by a passion for manufacturing and transparency. It's a business model that places the customer and their experience on a pedestal. It is something that provides an emotional connection and individualization. Those are two things that mass-produced products will never be able to offer. You cannot mechanize those in any facility. That's why the other products ship from a warehouse and DodoCase ships from a nest.

That Gut Feeling

If you keep your idea on paper, it will never succeed. It will sit on your desk and eventually serve as an impromptu mouse pad or a coaster.

If you keep your idea on paper, it will also start to tell you how high your chance of failure really is. Your idea will become *too* risky as you've been programmed to previously think of the word.

Successful ideas aren't bound to paper. They are subject only to analysis. Stop looking at your idea with the lens of a critic, and start feeling it with your gut. I call that intuition.

You can flip back through this book and list the ideas, products, or companies that I've mentioned on paper. Next to each of them, you could write down the variables that would doom them to fail. The reality is that they didn't fail, not in the larger sense of the term.

They succeeded because they were driven by a creative intuition. They were built on values. And the creator obsessed over them.

Values are things that are bigger than circumstance or situation. They transcend opportunity. Values drive a person to come up with their original idea. They drive that inventor to start the process of working on that idea. And values is the steam power behind launching that idea so that it can mesh with other people.

Now list all of the ideas, people, products, and businesses mentioned here, and write down the values that drove them to fruition. This will be a more comprehensive list.

It will also be more telling of what it takes to succeed when everything else is telling you that you can't.

What's At Your Core?

I was standing in a local Papa John's pizza restaurant waiting to pick up my carryout order. Looking around the place to kill time, I noticed a marbleized plaque prominently displayed on their front room wall.

It was the company's core values, the forces that drive and inspire everything they do. It included Focus, Accountability, Superiority, P.A.P.A., Attitude, and Constant Improvement. Each of these six values was further outlined on the plaque as well, and they are worth mentioning here.

Focus means constantly keeping the main thing the main thing. Decide what your main thing is and use it as an anchor to constantly calibrate your efforts.

Accountability means doing what we say we are going to do when we say we are going to do it. Papa John's version of accountability even mentions earning the right to hold others to a higher level of accountability through first expecting that level of themselves. If you have an idea and have decided to start it, you must be accountable to maintain it. Set up a structure for working on your art and use fidelity until it is launched.

Superiority is determined by the customer. Customer satisfaction must be consistent, quantifiable, and demonstrable. Once your idea is launched, how will you ensure that your customer or market is consistently satisfied?

P.A.P.A. stands for People Are Priority Always. Where superiority spotlights the people outside of the organization, P.A.P.A. focuses on the people within. This nationally recognized pizza chain realizes that their success depends on their ability, as a team, to work together to achieve their goals and expectations.

Whether you work alone or in an organization, you have a team. Who is yours?

Attitude is all about your thought process. If you think you can, or you think you can't, you're right. Other people will do a great job of trying to tear your ideas down. Those people are trolls. You have the responsibility of staying upbeat with a positive mental attitude. Your attitude is a reflection of what you value. Only you know what that is.

Constant Improvement means you cannot improve compared to the work of someone else. Improvement references your personal best only. Constant improvement means that you are always striving to top you. Papa John's core values make no mention of trying to outdo Pizza Hut, Dominos, or Little Caesar's. Papa John's isn't even the most successful Pizza Chain in the country. But they focus on constantly doing better than Papa John's has ever done before.

That makes them great.

So, What's At *Your* Core?

Those are Papa John's values. They're not yours. They're not Steve Jobs'. They're not Brian Scudamore's. They're not the Jacobs brothers' either. They might be similar, but core values come from you. They come from your core. And what lies at your core is passion.

What are you passionate about? That's what you will value. We obsess over the things we value. Values are the secret ingredient in our recipes for life.

If you use Papa John's values, you will fail. You're living someone else's story. That's not worth living. We all want you to live yours.

That's what you are most passionate about.

No one is passionate about Wal-Mart. We like their convenience, their low prices, and location. But Wal-Mart doesn't have a story worth telling. They have a story, but it ends by selling mediocrity.

Your story can't do that. Your story *needs* to spread. And you don't have to make it up. You're telling it right now. It's not important how it started. It's important how it ends.

Everyone loves a good ending.

Dave's Killer Bread

Dave Dahl's story spreads, and it has a happy ending. I'm positive that you will share it with someone after hearing about it. You might already know how it goes. Dave tells his story on the back of each loaf of Dave's Killer Bread that he sells, which has actually become quite a lot.

Dave Dahl grew up the son of a baker. He watched his father work. Relentless would describe what Dave saw. Unfortunately, Dave didn't have as much love for his dad as his father had for baking bread. So Dave turned to other things. He stole. He fought. He used meth. And Dave ended up in jail.

For 15 years.

For most people, that might as well be a life sentence. After all, there is a high return rate of felons who try to move on from the prison system.

Dave wanted to move on. He dreamt about what life would be like if he ever got through the life that he had created for himself as an inmate. Eventually, he did. And when he did, Dave Dahl went back to the family business where his brother had since taken over for their dad.

With the humility that can only result from prolonged adversity, Dave baked.

He didn't just bake like you or I bake. He created. He started by creating cookie lines that contained no trans fats or animal products. That was new for the company.

Then he created bread. Dave's bread is different. It's delicious! It's baked with the best organic materials available on the market, which is exactly where he launched his new idea.

Dave took Dave's Killer Bread to the Portland Farmer's Market in 2005. With samples of his bread for others to try and a determination to share his creation, Dave and his nephew stood under their canopy hocking bread to passersby by shouting, "Get your killer bread! Come try Dave's Killer Bread!"

And people did.

They tried it. They listened to Dave's story, and they connected with both.

His bread was so popular that the Portland Farmer's Market asked Dave's Killer Bread to become a permanent fixture in their local family. This was only a sign of things to come for Dave and his remarkable bread.

His story and the high quality of his product ultimately landed Dave's Killer Bread in stores throughout Oregon. Then Washington. Then Alaska. Now, the world.

What began as a four-time failure, trying to reclaim his life through a humble attempt at creating something of value, has turned into a brand that is now worth $50 million. That's a happy ending for Dave Dahl.

Go tell someone about Dave's story.

Flow

He should have failed. That's what it would have said about Dave the felon on paper. He should have relapsed to a life of drugs and crime and returned to prison. That's what most other felons do.

Dave thought otherwise.

When he rejoined his family's company, he didn't just bake. He fully committed himself to baking. He immersed himself in his art. He became fully engaged and engrossed in what he was doing, and that was creating bread. I'm sure that you've experienced this level of focus too. Not many of us know what to call it.

152

You might have heard it referred to as being in the zone. Sir Ken Robinson wrote a book about this and refers to this state of being as being in your element.

I call it *flow*.

Flow silences the lizard brain. When you are in flow, you are too taken up with what you are doing to notice anything else.

What gets you into flow isn't as important as just getting there. Whether it is reading, singing, mowing the lawn, running, reenacting Civil War battles, or anything else, do something that gets you to flow. It's almost as if devoting all of your mental energy to the task at hand opens the floodgates of passion which drowns the lizard brain's incessant yelling.

Suddenly, you forget about what could go wrong and become entirely driven by what is going right.

You can't coach flow. It's not something that results from a prescribed sequence of steps. It is the direct result of uninterrupted art. Flow enables remarkable idea generation not just *good-enough* brainstorming sessions. Flow helps us to see the possibilities. Flow allows us to view the world through the lens of an artist so that we start seeing possibility rather than dead ends.

This book has been written from 5 to 6:30 every single weekday morning since I decided to start writing it. You need to know that I'm not a morning person. Asked to wake up that early for anything else, I would have fought you over it and won. But each morning as I climb the stairs to the quiet of the loft in my house, I get excited to open my laptop and begin writing once again. It has breathed life into what I do throughout the rest of my day.

I research and type with little awareness of time passing by. I ponder and start digging. Left to my ability to manage myself, I would write until there were no more ideas left in me. That's why I set an alarm. It forces me to stop writing and get ready for the day. I resent it every single time it happens, but it's not the alarm's fault. For me, writing drowns out the lizard brain.

I'm in flow. No one ever wants to leave that.

Never Listen to a Troll

No matter what it is that you create, you won't be able to replicate the experience of creating it. You won't be able to make flow for someone else. Paradoxically, we aim to create the most value that we can for those whom we reach while knowing that they won't experience the level of value that we, ourselves, did when we started our ideas.

Those whom we reach can find their own way to flow while engrossed in your materialized idea though. You just won't be able to include instructions on how to get them there.

Then again, some people won't. They will give up and turn back too soon.

Scour any page of Amazon listings, look at the reviews on Foursquare or Yelp, and peruse the comments thread on a blog post. You will see a lot of positive experiences. These make us feel good. Undoubtedly punctuated throughout them are the trolls.

Trolls are ugly. They're grotesque. Trolls are so passé that they cannot stand things that are naturally beautiful, so they wait for the right moment to attack. Trolls have one intent, to hurt you to the point that you stop making art.

It's easy to spot a troll. They're the ones who criticize ideas, products, services, or people and then quickly run back to their safe hiding places. Trolls do not suggest solutions. They do not care about them. Trolls simply set fire and run away.

In the context of blog post comments, theirs are anonymous.

Their Amazon product reviews focus on how the distributor fell short on *everything*. They tend to generalize their dislike for a product or piece of art as how everyone else must feel as well. This doesn't just happen on Amazon. It's not just online either. It happens at work, at school, at church, in the news, at the gym, at the gas station, and at family reunions.

Accept it now that trolls are everywhere. They are insecure about their ability to create, so they humiliate attempts by those around them instead. Trolls are wrong. They always are. Thankfully, the only people who ever listen to their cynicism are other trolls and their victims.

You are most likely not a troll. You will be a victim, that is, if you're not one already.

When you are targeted by a troll, recognize him or her for who he or she is, an ugly, ugly troll. Consider the source, let them grumble from under their bridge, and then jump back into flow.

The Happiness Factor

You can be happy without being in flow. But you cannot be in flow without being happy. Happiness is the secret ingredient when it comes to launching your idea. If it doesn't immediately make you happy, ditch it. Doing something that does not make you happy is not worth your investment of time, energy, or apathy. It's a dead end, and you are not.

Remember that emotional labor scales. The spirit with which you create will be broadcast to your market not only in the quality of execution, but in the way that you talk to them about it. If you can't talk about what you do with fury, then others won't care to talk about it either. That's why I love the stories that I have shared here. The passion and happiness behind each of them are more interesting to me than the ideas they feature.

Being happy about what you do will free your mind to indulge in how to best do it. Your creativity will shine.

Joy in the process of concocting an idea, starting the work of making it come to life, and launching it into the world are success. If you do that well then your idea catching traction is a bonus. The experience of creating will have the greatest return of all. It returns bliss, delirium, elation, felicity, glee, jubilation, and pleasure.

No one else can make you happy. Nothing else can give you happiness. Happiness resides where your passion meets the drafting table and time fades away. It thrives on breathing oxygen, on seeing the sunshine, and on finally meeting you. So let it.

Happiness creates flow. And flow creates happiness.

There's no entropy, or lost energy in this design.

The Precipice of Failure

You might be on the hunt for flow. It's out on the furthest reach of the tree's limb. That's where the branch bends the most. It's where the branch sways the most. And it's where very few people are. Go out on it. It's the precipice of failure, where things could go one way or they could go another. Flow is where we've been told to never journey because it's too dangerous for us to stand.

There's no real danger where flow is, at least, not if you're willing to accept toppling down either side of the mountain.

Is it safe, or is it interesting?

Our response to how we answer this will determine how high we are willing to climb, and what we willfully do. If it's safe, it's already been done. On the off chance that it hasn't, no one is going to pay attention to it. There is no drama. We are enamored by drama.

If it's interesting, that opens up a whole new world of opportunity. In the territory of interesting lies adventure, novelty, newness, innovation, passion, failure, happiness, and flow.

You cannot fail with a safety net. By staying in your safety zone, you already have. There's no risk to be taken. Art without a harness is what truly takes our breath away. It is dramatic. It has pull. It is extraordinary and unusual. In one word, making art outside of your safety zone is remarkable.

One such place that we do this is the sky.

Taking Flight

We have been trying to fly since cavemen were running around, flapping their arms, and chasing flocks of birds. Taking to the skies is overcoming our limitations. Mankind was not created with the physical ability to fly, so we try that much harder to do it.

Back through prehistory there is evidence through art that flight was something we sought. Winged humanoids on cavernous walls have continued to evolve through the art, stories, and myths that drive our culture today.

We share these stories because they tell something about us. They tell us about what we can do. They don't tell us to do the impossible, but if we listen to them close enough they invite us to do it.

Some of the smartest, wealthiest, most revered people throughout history have tried to figure out how to conquer flight. They didn't do it for the money. They didn't do it for the fame. They did it because everyone said it was impossible. Everyone except them.

The Flying Monk

Eilmer of Malmesbury was a monk with a fire in his belly for adventure. He lived during the 11th Century, and set out to do what no man had successfully done before, fly. Having observed the birds for some time, Eilmer fashioned a set of wings out of bird feathers and fitted them to his arms and legs.

Then Eilmer climbed to the top of a tower at Malmesbury Abbey.

With an audience of onlookers below, this adventuresome monk spread his wings out wide and jumped out into the uncertain air. Surprising to all, Eilmer flew. And then he didn't. He soared roughly 200 meters before losing control of himself in the winds and quickly falling with a crash to the ground.

Eilmer did not die. He did break both of his legs which would render him crippled for the rest of his life. Notwithstanding, the inability to walk did not deter him.

Instead, Eilmer studied his failed attempt at gliding through the clouds and analyzed what went well and what of course went wrong. *What did the birds have that he did not?*

A tail. He had not engineered a tail. That was it!

A tail would help him to control the turbulent air. Every flying creature has one. Having discovered what he could not have known without his first failure, Eilmer designed a glider with a smoothly engineered tail.

He was ready to risk his life to try it again.

Unfortunately, the abbot at Malmesbury Abbey was not so willing, and he refused to let Eilmer jump off his church a second time.

What a Waste

Wrong. Eilmer's attempt at manned flight didn't end in him flying more than a furlong. That's true. Without Eilmer's successful furlong flight, those who travelled two furlongs and further wouldn't have had Eilmer's experience and insight to build on. It would have been fortuitous.

DaVinci's flying machines had Eilmer's tail. So did Gusmamao's. Otto Lilienthal's, the Wright's, and the company who built the airplane that you could possibly be reading this book in right now have them too.

Each iteration offered new expertise from their more advanced failed attempts to perfect human flight.

So now, we soar.

We Fly Because We Failed

Talk to anyone passionate about human flight, and ask them why they care so much about taking off from the ground. Inevitably it will come back to one of the earliest failed attempts at flying.

Icarus.

In Greek mythology, Daedalus and his son, Icarus, needed to escape from the island of Crete after angering King Minos. Having been banished to the Labyrinth that Daedalus, himself, designed for the King, he created sets of wings made of yarn, wax and feathers for himself and his son.

Before taking off, Daedalus gave Icarus the cautionary imperative to not fly too closely to the sun or too low to the sea, but to follow Daedalus' path.

After escaping the inescapable, Icarus found himself sucking the marrow out of flight as he climbed higher and higher into the sky. Yet sooner than later, he realized that what he was flapping was not his hand-crafted set of wings. It was his naked arms. Having disregarding his father's warning, Icarus flew too closely to the sun, and the wax from his wings had melted. Arms flailing, Icarus plummeted to his death in what is now known as the Icarian Sea (named after this maverick of exploration).

Choose the moral that you want. Regardless, Icarus failed first. That's why we've continued to take flight.

This story is a myth. But so is your belief that you are stuck where you are. Successful flight began with a series of failures, leaps of faith, and new designs.

Fashion your wings, and fly. Over and over and over.

Nothing to Gain From the Ground

The ground is our safety zone. We cannot fall if our feet are firmly planted on the floor. We cannot fly if we are stagnant either. Naturally, there will be very few who are willing to try. The risk of shame is too great. There is a chance that we will fall. A risk like this far outweighs the risk of succeeding.

Except for a few of us.

That is why the Wright Brothers were the only ones with a flying machine at Kitty Hawk. They were the only ones with enough chutzpah to try.

The part of the story that we're never taught is the criticism that Orville and Wilbur received for believing they could do what no one else had managed to do themselves. If you think they had the support of the masses behind them, they did. They just didn't have it until after they took flight.

What person brave enough to pioneer a new idea has ever had the support of the masses beforehand? None until they proved the impossible possible.

The Wright Brothers were not popularized because they tried. They were neither popular at the time as they tried. Their fan club jumped on their bandwagon once they succeeded.

Oh, there were already people behind the hubris of the Wrights. They were just the minority, a cadre of believers who had overcome their lizard brains to support innovation. We call people like this the first followers. Nothing matters without them.

Nothing.

You're Not Trying to Reach the World

First followers are the people who catch your vision. They are the ones who will take your idea and run with it when no one else cares to take a chance on you. They were the disciples of Christ. They were the first to reach Jamestown. They were the first to move West. And the first to buy iPods.

This is the Age of Connection. Those who make the connections for us are the first followers. They're the sparks in the dry grass. The imperfection in the dyke. The grit in the finely calibrated machine.

Get your idea to them. Let them take it and run. Watch the rest respond to it later. No one else matters right now. If you are trying to reach the world, you're not going to reach anyone worth reaching. Set your sights on the first followers, and then never lose focus of them.

It's not that the rest don't see the value in what you have created. It's that they want to see it succeed before leaving their safety zone to latch on. The first followers couldn't care less about their safety zone. They care about new, better, remarkable, innovative.

First followers are the most passionate about you. They'll get obsessed.

And of course, being obsessed spreads. Obsession is highly contagious.

It spreads more than the disrespect from outside your market. Expect your idea to be disrespected. Therein lies a principle of success, target those within your market and ignore those who are not part of it. If someone tries to shame you or criticize your work, they're not who you should be sharing your ideas with in the first place. They might come around later, but that's within their control, not yours.

Love Hurts

If you're willing to catapult your idea, then you obviously love what you have created. You couldn't get that far with something than didn't fill you to the brim with excitement. Executing an idea is harder than coming up with it no matter what your idea is. It requires vision, determination, resiliency, pain, uncertainty, passion, and joy. Going through this gauntlet isn't worth the time of someone who is not emotionally invested in his or her art. You can't make it if you aren't.

Unfortunately, as you execute the plans you have for the ideas that you have created, you are the only one emotionally invested in them. At least at first. It's how you reflect your commitment for your art that will begin to connect your ideas with the emotions of others. When this happens, people will care. They will care enough to buy. They will care enough to share. The will care enough to take what you've made and ally themselves with it.

Still, most won't care to care. That's perfectly okay.

If you are setting out to convert everyone to your way of thinking, you are going to lose. There will be those who resist and reject your way of thinking. They won't "get" your worldview. They might even go as far as publicly criticizing your efforts and passion. Can you handle that?

Of course you can.

It's your lizard brain telling you that you can't. Your lizard brain isn't part of what makes you who you are. It's a leftover remnant of a more dangerous existence, a life in the Serengeti. A life without a home. A life where warring tribes wanted everything that you had and were willing to kill you for it.

It's finally your turn to kill for something.

It kills to see a negative jab on a comment thread. It kills to hear someone talking about how your idea is worthless or drab. It kills to see Tweets or posts about how someone failed to connect with your idea and generalized it as a waste.

The problem is not you. And it is not your idea. The problem is that someone else did not connect with what you have to offer. That's their problem, not yours. Don't take on more than you can by making it your problem to deal with. Your problem is ensuring that you don't give up on your passion. Your problem is to stay obsessed and contagious. Your problem, your only problem is to fail and make it count.

Target your passion at a niche audience, not the world. A niche gets you. The world has a hard time getting anything. Just look at our popular media and sources of entertainment, then decide whether the world's opinion is one that resonates with you. I really hope it isn't.

The world needs something new. They're not going to ask you for it. They're not even going to expect that it is coming, nor will they anticipate that it will come from you. But it will. It must.

You owe it to the world. You owe it to us, that is unless you're a fan of *Jersey Shore*.

If It Isn't Hurting, Call for Help

The art of creating, of being creative, and of executing your creativity hurts. It hurts a lot. It starts hurting when you begin thinking outside of the box. It hurts to think of new ways of doing things. Once you've managed to do that, it hurts to think about starting work on your new project. Then it hurts to go back and evaluate what you've done.

There's a barrage of thoughts, an air-raid of missiles being launched back and forth in your mind. And they explode.

This isn't going to work. (Boom!)

But I really think it's new and inventive. (Crack!)

Your ideas aren't worth anything. (Bang!)

I need to find a new solution. (Crash!)

Who are you? (Crash!)

Exactly that, I'm me. (Bang!)

It would be too scary. Just spend your time and energy on what you are sure about. (Whizz!)

Well, I'm not sure about anything. (Fizz!)

It never stops. This smattering of self-criticism is good.

It's the sign that you've started something worth doing. You've started something valuable and new. It's dangerous and exciting. It's refreshing. Your lizard brain is telling you to stay away from this constantly, and it will never cease to scream at you.

Tell it *thanks* and then get started.

Here come the stomach aches. On come the sweats. Welcome the sleepless nights and the irritability. These aren't symptoms of wasted time. They diagnose something worth fretting about. Your idea might just work. It might inspire and connect with others. It might fall flat on its face along the way. But if it wasn't worth doing, you wouldn't get far enough to see that happen anyway.

Embrace the pains of passion. They hurt. They throb. If you don't feel them, you're not passionate enough about your idea. If you stop feeling them, you've lost all your passion.

Whatever you do, don't wish away the hurt. It means that you're actually making a difference. And a difference is exactly what the world needs.

Steve Knows This

No book about failing your way to success can be without at least a couple mentions of Steve Jobs. He did not set out to become one of the greatest inventors of our generation. He just followed his love. So here is another Jobs story.

When Steve Jobs entered Reed College in Portland, Oregon, he had no idea what he wanted to do with his life. He began taking the courses that were prescribed for him, but after six months of college he did not see any value in the path he was set on. Steve also felt that he was wasting his parents' life savings on tuition. So, Steve Jobs dropped out.

Most people assume that Jobs left campus to pursue his muse that would later become Apple. It wasn't quite so. Steve dropped out of college so that he could drop-in instead. Now that he was not a formal student, Jobs was free to audit the classes that he actually wanted to attend. He was free to indulge in the topics that piqued his curiosity.

One of these was Calligraphy. There was no practical application for calligraphy in Steve Jobs' life, he admitted that, but the art of this stylized writing interested him, so he took the class. Unlike the general education classes Steve had taken before, he loved every minute of Calligraphy and obsessed over it. He continued to drop-in on classes at Reed College for about another 18 months before leaving campus for good.

Starting anew, Steve took a job with Atari. He travelled to India to learn more about Zen Buddhism. He spent a while tripping on LSD. About four years after Jobs walked away from Reed College, he started a project with a friend named Steve Wozniak, which would turn out to be the biggest trip of his life.

The two tech geeks set up shop in Steve's parents' garage on Crist Drive in Los Altos, California, and they started building and selling one of Wozniak's recent inventions upon Jobs' enthusiastic recommendation. They called it the Apple I computer, and at age 20, Steve Jobs' affair with Apple was born.

Ten years later, Jobs found himself in charge of a company worth $2 billion. By that point, Apple had grown in every sense of the word. Out of necessity, Jobs brought on additional players to help his company scale. One of these individuals was a man named John Sculley. Steve had lured him away from Pepsi-Cola to serve as Apple's CEO.

It was an excellent move until it wasn't.

Jobs and Sculley's vision for Apple began to diverge. Conflict arose, and Apple's Board of Directors sided with Sculley. Steve Jobs was fired from the company that he started, going from the top of the world to rock bottom.

And it hurt.

How could something like this have possibly happened. Just imagine the shame.

Jobs would later say that being fired from Apple was the best thing that could have possibly happened to him.

Ludicrous, isn't it? At least, it sounds that way. Being fired from the multi-billion dollar company that you started, being the best thing that could have possibly happened to you?

Steve didn't label it a failure. He labeled it an opportunity. No wonder he would continue to be so successful.

That's exactly what it was, an opportunity. Being fired from Apple was an opportunity for Steve Jobs to be humbled. It was an opportunity for him to recalibrate. It was particularly a great opportunity to start over.

He didn't run and hide from the industry that he loved. Oh, he thought about it. That would have been the easiest thing to do. Can you imagine the world of personal computing if Steve Jobs had run away?

No, he stayed and started anew.

Jobs started a company called NeXT. Targeting a different market than Apple had set out to inspire, NeXT was a computer company creating computer workstations designed for business markets and higher education. One of their greatest ideas was something called NeXTSTEP. It was an object-oriented operating system.

Jobs and NeXT later decided to drop out of the computer hardware business to focus more on software development and marketing the successor to NeXTSTEP, which Jobs called OPENSTEP.

Around this same time, Steve Jobs bought a division of Lucasfilm known as the Graphics Group and made it his own company as well. What Jobs would do with this project would soon be realized as moviegoers everywhere were introduced to a cowboy named Woody and a spaceman named Buzz.

Steve took the Graphics Group and created Pixar.

As for NeXT, Jobs sold the company. The check that the initial investors took to the bank was for $429 million. The best part of the story is the company that wrote the check. Ironically, it was Apple Inc.

Jobs was given 1.5 million Apple shares for selling NeXT and their OPENSTEP software which would later inspire the OSX operating system that catapulted Apple computers into the winning position of the computer wars. Jobs was asked to come back to Apple as a consultant and, within the same year was hired as interim CEO. Three years later, in 2000, the interim tag was removed, making Steve Jobs the CEO of Apple Inc., the company that he started in his parents' garage.

Isn't it a good thing that he didn't run away?

Seeing Dots

His was the most public failure of the time, but Steve refused to accept it as that. He refused to accept the shame that came but instead moved out of his comfort zone. His comfort zone said run away, so Jobs sent his comfort zone packing.

There was no way that he could have seen where this attitude would take him. You might be in the same place.

Standing at the edge of uncertainty, there is no possible way to see where your life and art will take you. You will certainly move. Forward, perhaps. But connecting the dots beforehand is impossible.

It's uncomfortable to realize this as the truth. But you have to. No one in this book has been able to connect the dots from the outset. Yet, they've all been able to connect them once they looked back. The fog in the crystal ball clears once you've walked around to the other side. Things seem less serious too.

Challenges make more sense once they have happened. We can see more transparently once everything is in place. There is no risk when we look backward, only sense. Our failures make sense in the rearview mirror. Jobs would certainly agree with that. So would every kid who's ever seen a CGI animated film, or every designer who has ever used a Mac.

But the dots would never have been connected had there not been a willingness to move forward into the shadow of failure. As you look at the opportunity that lays in front of you, you can either view it as an uncertain risk or an opportunity. How you choose to view it will most certainly determine what you do.

Before you make up your mind, however, know this: the world we live in was not made by people who ran away from risk. The world we live in was made by those who ran headfirst into it screaming from the top of their lungs.

Just Like us

These people have no superpowers. Superpowers don't exist. In fact, the most exciting superheroes are the ones who are subject to weakness. They are fallible.

Nobody within these pages was born with a great idea or spoon fed success. They didn't grow up in the same neighborhood. They didn't graduate from the same school. And none of them went to a secret summer academy for the future famous. Looking back, none of them even came from a family of wealth. If they did, they surely chose to reject it.

The one thing that all of these people have in common is that they were willing to pursue their passions.

Passion isn't store-bought. You cannot take a college course or read a book to figure out how to get it. It is available to each of us. But passion isn't free.

It costs you in commitment. It costs you in fear. It costs you in time, and energy, and art. These are all things that are scary to sacrifice. Why do something that makes you so scared? Or so tired? Or so late? Why do something that has never been done before?

Because when we do, we are telling the world that *we lived*.

Hiding in the eaves of safety is not living. It is existing. There are plenty of people who wake up every day and simply exist. They hate what they do, and people can tell that.

There are far less, and not enough, who wake up and live.

The Last Lecture

Randy Pausch decided to live once he realized he was going to die. He didn't do it to write a best-selling book, but what he commenced doing would inspire one that connected with enough people to make it a New York Times best-seller.

Randy's big idea, his art, was life.

On September 18, 2007, Randy Pausch, a computer science professor at Carnegie Mellon University, walked into a lecture hall before an audience of 400 people at Carnegie Mellon and shared the story of finding out, quite recently, that cancer had taken control of his pancreas and would in a matter of months take his life.

This was the beginning of Pausch's last lecture titled *Really Achieving Your Childhood Dreams*. While most last lectures are customarily designed to impart any wisdom you would give to your students if you knew it would be your last chance to do so, Pausch's last lecture was not about them.

It was about his own children who were still very young. He wanted them to know that their dad lived and how he hoped they would choose to live as well.

He spoke to the maximum capacity crowd of his childhood, his dreams, his fears, and his ambitions. He narrated how he became a Disney Imagineer after a series of rejections. He told of experiencing zero gravity after a sequence of setbacks. He told of the joy that he had and the life that he still loved, none of which came easily.

In his last lecture, Randy Pausch reminded us that,

The brick walls are there for a reason. The brick walls are not there to keep us out. The brick walls are there to give us a chance to show how badly we want something. Because the brick walls are there to stop the people who don't want it badly enough. They're there to stop the other people.

Randy Pausch lost his battle with pancreatic cancer just 10 months later at the age of 47. His story has inspired millions.

It's not inspiring because of the timing of his death. It's not inspiring because of his career or prestige. I wouldn't even say that it is inspiring because of the specific things that he accomplished in his short life. What I think truly inspires us about Randy Pausch and *The Last Lecture* is that it reminds us of ourselves.

It makes us face our finite lives. What are we capable of achieving? This was Randy's idea.

He worked to show his children, and incidentally the rest of the world, that anything is attainable as long as you truly work for it. Simply working hard enough or long enough isn't enough. You have to work passionately. This love of life is what helps some to get past the brick walls while others get discouraged and give up.

How badly do you want your ideas to succeed? How many walls are you willing to overcome? There will be a lot. But when it boils down to it, walls are all that stand between us and fulfilling our dreams. And most of those walls are the Lizard.

Every wall has a top. You *can* climb over it. Every wall has an end. You *can* go around it. Every wall has imperfections. You *can* go through them. You just might not realize what you can do if you're standing at the bottom of the wall.

How badly do you want it? Then start climbing.

Stop Paying Attention

Watching someone climb the wall is not going to do you any good. Watching someone execute will profit you nothing. Watching an artist create his art is a fun thing to do. But once it is done, you've created nothing, and the artist has had all of the fun. You need to stop paying so much attention to what everyone else is doing and do something yourself.

When we are captivated by awe, it changes what we see. It shapes our perceptions of things. But we are not changing anything. We are what is being changed.

The act of creating is much different from the act of watching. It is when we jump in and start creating art that we become a participant instead of a spectator. We start learning instead of watching. And when we learn how to do something new, we become directors of our lives.

Hundreds of thousands of spectators are not going to gather for your idea. You're not going to sell tickets to your process. It might catch on with a crowd after its launch, but not until then. You need to have a different driving force to create art. Something that you can control. Money, fame, and even success are beyond your reach while creating.

Enjoyment, though, isn't.

The very best ideas were not born to make millions. They were generated out of a love for joy. Joy isn't a state of contentment. It's a feeling of great pleasure and happiness. Starting your idea will surely be an experience that brings you great pleasure and happiness. So start.

You won't know whether it succeeds or fails until the process of creating is over. It's truly the process of creating your art that brings you joy. By simply doing, you are experiencing feelings of great pleasure and happiness. How could you not label this as success?

Gesundheit

The joy of the process is lived by a man I once met by the name of Hunter Adams. You might know him as "Patch."

I was in high school, and Patch was speaking at a local university. I remember nothing about what he said that evening, and everything about how he oozed joy. Upon first glancing at him I quickly noticed the earring he was wearing. It was a fork, an actual, straight-from-the utensil-drawer fork. It complimented his clown suit quite well.

Patch Adams is a clown. He's a physician too. Having graduated with his Doctor of Medicine degree from Virginia Commonwealth University, Patch set out to do something different. He wanted to innovate, he wanted change. Most of all he wanted connection.

He became a doctor to connect with his patients, not to simply cure them.

Patch had this idea long before entering VCU. From a very young age, Patch Adams hurt. He hurt not from the ailments of a broken body, but from the ailments of a broken heart. He lacked joy in his childhood and was the victim of intense bullying.

As a result, this future visionary actively pursued suicide more than once during his high school years and was temporarily hospitalized for it. It was during this time that he created his big idea.

Having tried to end his life three times in one year, Patch decided, "you don't kill yourself, stupid; you make a revolution."

His revolution would take place in the arena of healthcare, a field that has been constrained by business, insurance companies, and fear of malpractice lawsuits.

Hunter "Patch" Adams used medicine as a vehicle for social change. He created a facility known as The Gesundheit Institute, on principles that mainstream healthcare providers avoided. The principles that Patch chose to follow brought him joy, indirectly bringing his patients experiences of great pleasure in the face of great pain and hurt.

His principles are his values. And here they are.

The first principle that The Gesundheit Institute was built on is that there is no charge for the care. Patients receive needed treatment for absolutely free. The idea is to eliminate debt in the medical interaction so that caregivers can begin recreating human community. Patch and his staff give care, not so people feel like they owe him something, but so they feel like they belong to something.

Another principle foundational to Patch's idea is that The Gesundheit Institute has nothing to do with malpractice insurance. The fear of messing up has crippled mainstream medical interactions. It has set up a barrier between caregivers and their patients.

Vulnerability is embodied by Patch's revolution. Clearly aware that he can only offer caring without the promise of a cure, Patch Adams reserves the right to make mistakes so that he is free to trust and be trusted.

Patch believes that the wellbeing of the staff is as important as the wellbeing of the patients. This is the value of customer experience and authentic human connection. What patients want more than treatment is compassion and attention. Isn't that what we all want whether sick or not? This is a call for time. Those giving time are caregivers. If they are not well, how can they connect with their patients?

One more principle that Patch's revolution is based on was discovered by the time spent actually connecting with his patients. Imagine that. The majority of the adults he connected with lacked a day-to-day vitality for life. Patch defines this as good health. The majority of these people were missing the very same thing, engagement. So Patch brings them vitality. He might be best known for integrating medicine with performing arts, arts and crafts, agriculture, nature, education, recreation and social service. This can be prescribed freely without the fear of side effects. The only possible side effect from such treatment is joy with instances of obsession.

Patch Adams cannot guarantee that his patients will return to full health. No one really can. In fact, there is very little in life that we can guarantee. Still, he helps them to return to good health, which is health of the heart and mind. Patch treats patients from his heart by sharing himself with them. He connects.

When we're willing to give part of ourselves away to each person we interact with, we are not left with nothing. We return with more than we could have possibly started with. More than we had before we connected. More than we were before starting.

This is not failure. This is joy. What is the end result of your art again?

By All Means Paint

Vincent Van Gogh addressed the baneful lizard brain with his art. He said, "If you hear a voice within you say 'you cannot paint,' then by all means paint, and that voice will be silenced."

That's at the root of all of this. By all means paint. Build. Write. Dance. Invest. Design. Program. Sing. Film. Blog. Run. Start. Finish. Launch.

If there is not a voice telling you that you cannot do it, then it is not going to be worth doing. Someone has already done it.

No one is going to knock on your door and ask you if you have any good ideas. You're not going to get discovered. You are the one making discoveries. And the best time to start creating is over. Start now instead. People are counting on you to do it.

One Final Story

It's about Mr. Dave.

Mr. Dave loved kids that no one else loved. He had committed his life to working with forgotten children. Kids who had joined gangs, sold drugs, beat up their moms and themselves.

Adults didn't call him Mr. Dave. Just the kids. He worked with them in group homes, detention centers, and behavioral rehabilitation facilities. Most of these kids didn't even come from the state that Mr. Dave lived in. They were typically shipped away to get fixed, often from inner cities.

There wasn't anything wrong with them. They just made bad choices. That was Mr. Dave's mentality. That's why he treated them like people, exactly like he would treat you or me. He loved connecting with his kids and would often do it over a chess board. It's very doubtful that any of them ever beat him, but they all kept coming to play with Mr. Dave.

Until they couldn't play with him anymore.

Mr. Dave's passion for his work had taken him to the pinnacle of his field, CEO of his own behavioral clinic. At the same time that Mr. Dave's career was escalating, his health was declining. It wasn't the result of anything he did, at least not that science knows about.

Mr. Dave was suffering from Amyotrophic Lateral Sclerosis (ALS), otherwise known as Lou Gehrig's Disease. ALS is a disease of the nerve cells in the brain and spinal cord that control voluntary muscle movement. Slowly, but surely, a person with ALS starts to experience muscular atrophy. Their muscles slowly stop working and die.

Mr. Dave, once six and a half feet tall and weighing over 350 pounds, now stood like a hermit. His body was wasting away. His hair was graying and thinning. And the cane that kept him upright eventually couldn't do it any longer.

After falling one too many times, Mr. Dave was consigned to a wheelchair.

I received a call from Mr. Dave one evening, very unexpectedly. I was on vacation in New York City and at the time of the call was just getting my ticket ripped for one of the final home baseball games in the old Yankees Stadium.

"I'm not going to be able to talk to you for very long", he told me. Just entering the stadium, I was thinking the same thing about myself.

"I'm at the hospital. My lungs are collapsing, and I'm about to go into emergency tracheotomy surgery. The doctor said that I will lose my ability to talk for good." I was stunned. Someone who had undeniably been put on this earth to talk to people was now telling me that I would never hear his voice again.

There was only one thing I could think of to say. "I love you, Dad." And the conversation ended.

Mr. Dave had touched the lives of so many kids. The one he touched the deepest was mine. He was my father, and I emulated him. I still do and always will.

I spent most of the Yankees game that night on the phone arranging a red-eye flight to take me from New York City to Tampa, Florida where my dad was hospitalized. I got there early the next morning. At first glance, I did what any boy would do to their father. I ran up to his bed to say hello.

But he couldn't say it back. All he could do was wave at me. And even that was quite shaky.

He had a tube in his throat, not down his mouth, but literally in his throat, and more wires connected to him than a circuit board.

My dad remained in the hospital for roughly three months receiving treatment and therapy to help him to preserve the functionality that he still had. Over the course of those months, he miraculously got his voice back, something that I still don't understand to this day.

He had been flown by medical plane to a hospital in Utah where his extended family was from. My father had made such great improvements that the doctors, both in Utah and Florida, told him that he was capable enough to have his life back.

With the help of a home health nurse, my dad was released from the hospital and into his younger sister's care. She had a large enough home for him to move into with the equipment that the hospital had sent him with. He would need every last piece of it.

I lived with my wife in Idaho at the time when my dad called me again. He had made it to his sister's home and was relaxing in his wheelchair in front of a live broadcast of a University of Utah football game, another of his passions. My dad had been out of the hospital for only a few hours, but he was already enjoying the comforts of life before he had his tracheotomy.

The conversation was short. Physically, he couldn't talk for very long and soon needed to give his body a rest. But it ended with "I love you" and "I'll see you real soon".

That would be the last time I ever heard my dad's voice.

While getting help from his sister as he got ready the next morning, my dad's heart stopped beating without warning. Apparently, he didn't even look like he was in pain before he slumped over onto the ground and stopped breathing. He was without oxygen just long enough for him to fall into a coma.

The ambulance came, and he was rushed to the nearest hospital where he was put on life support long enough for everyone to say their goodbyes. And everyone did. Everyone but me.

I was racing down to Utah after getting the call from my uncle where he told me that there had been an accident with my dad. But he died before I could make it there.

On the first day that my father was told that he was going to live, he died. Mr. Dave was 45 years old.

The Moral at the End of the Book

Mr. Dave's art was connecting with kids who needed someone to connect with. Though for much shorter of a time than he had initially planned, he did exactly that.

I told you his story. I've told you many stories of people who have acted on their ideas and created their art.

So, what's mine?

My idea was to write a book. I wanted to write a book that would connect with people, not everyone, but real people. I wanted to write it about those who have connected with me.

This is my book. This is my art. This is my vulnerability. This is me walking into the gaping void of uncertainty where failure and success both loom. This is me out on a limb.

I'm okay with whatever happens because I know that whatever may come is not the end of the road. Failing is a part of success. It is a part of art. It is a part of living. It is a part of death. If you cannot fail, it doesn't count. Writing this book and sharing it with you counts. It definitely counts.

Your turn.

Thank You

I would like to thank my friend John Hardison for taking the time to read over the manuscript for this book when it was still in its infant form. I asked him to review what I had written, thinking that he would just tell me if it sounded good. He did that and a lot more. John put each line under a microscope and doctored the grammar, punctuation, and usage that I either did not notice or was not technically aware about. That is remarkable service.

It is nice to have someone as passionate as John to share my ideas with. He is a remarkable person and friend.

Thanks, John.

Dave Guymon is a son, a husband, and a father. These are what he tries to do best. *If You Can't Fail, It Doesn't Count* is the first book he has written. Writing is what he tries to do next best.

Visit Dave's blog at www.DaveGuymon.com.